HOW SOCIAL ENVIRONMENT INFLUENCES

EMPLOYEES BEHAVIORAL CHANGE

JOHN LOK

Copyright © John Lok
All Rights Reserved.

Contents

Preface

Preface

My reader can image you are one business scientist to enter one marketing, economic and human resource departments journey in any organizations. Your aim need to solve any challenges when you encounter in your business journey. This book explains why organizations need to find any new strategy to develop human resource management plan in order to raise employee productivity and improve efficiency when they feel social environment is changing.

This book concerns my recommendation how entreprensur chooses to achieve whose marketing or/and economy or / and human resource strategy to achieve to raise organizational more efficiency and effectiveness. I shall indiate why some UK and US some large business organizations whose weakness and strengths to cause whose organizations inefficient and I shall explain why and how social changing environment may influence marketing environment changes.

Prologue

How to apply behavioral economic

principles to make any business

strategy

Behavioural economy and business

strategy relationship p.121-151

Chapter 2
How labor behavior influences
efficiency
How utility maximization,
equilibrium and efficiency concepts
influence employee's individual behavior

Costs and benefits analysis concept

measures consumer's individual or

employee's individual behavior

Preferences over risky and
uncertain outcomes of individual
behavior economic theories.

What is behavioral game theory?

How entrepreneur applys
behavioral economic strategy to do
decision
    Why does consumer psychology
and economy environment has clos
relationship p.152-182

Chapter 3
Why social behavior may influence organizational strategy needs to be changed

Human Behavioral network job brings social
economic benefits
What does human network job mean
Why human network job behavior may influence economy

Robots take our jobs behavioral and economy influences
Robot job behavior brings economy influences

Intellectual human economic behaviors
What does intellectual human economic behaviors
mean ?
The relationship between social change and human
behavior
How human productive behavior may influence economic development

● New Zealand farmer individual wine productive behavior
● America high technological productive behavior
● China share market investing behavior
Why has any individual country have many people invest share behavior which can influence the country's macro consumption desire?
Can technology influence human shopping behavioral change?
Why and how human behavior may influence the country's economic growth or recession?
Technology how impacts human behavior changing?
How and why employees behaviors may influence economy development?
Robots invention whether they can help organizations to raise efficiencies or inefficiencies?
Why social behavior may influence organizational strategy needs to be changed ? p.183-240
Chapter 4
What are organizational hard and soft skills
● Skills shortages on developing
country market

ONE
ONLINE KNOWLEDGEABLE JOBS RAISED PRODUCTIVE METHODS

Entrepreneur will face knowledge productivity environment change and labor need challenges. Nowadays, enterprise competition is serious. Entrepreneur needs to change employees' productivity methods to raise employee efficiency.

In what way has globalization affected employers choose online work to provide to local or overseas to raise productivity? Is online work still a useful working place environment for local and overseas employers to raise productivity in a globalized online age, such as online electronic books' authors, online office administration or online surveys or online researchers etc. kind of online jobs supplying?

Our age is entering an online business environment, such as online electronic air tickets sale, online electronic books publishing, online advertising and online shopping and website design service promotion , online university education etc. different kind of online businesses from internet. It seems online channel can increase global online job chances to affect that our live and our job nature to be changed every day. For example, online electronic book publishing business will be popular, many different countries' readers who like to buy electronic books to study, due to these online electronic book shops, e.g. Amazon, lulu, book Rix, book tango etc. electronic book stores which can provide free charge to deliver cheaper paper books to any overseas countries' readers' homes and which paper book prices are more cheaper to compare to book shops' paper books process after who have paid to buy any electronic books or paper books from these online book stores websites. Moreover, these readers can read these book stores' electronic books from online publishing sellers' websites to download these electronic books to study at homes or any libraries etc. computer provision of places easily and conveniently. So readers do not need to walk to any book shops to buy any paper books and who also do not need to bring any heavy paper books back to homes conveniently. Hence, electronic publishers can provide electronic book authors' job chances to write their books and type to computers to register to be online authors to publish whose electronic or paper books to earn loyalty income at home very easily. Also, the globalizing online job nature can change the customized office work style. It won't need staffs go to office to work from 9:00 AM to 6:00 PM. In general office workers need to spend eight to ten working hours with five or six working days within per week commonly. Hence, online office workers don't need to pay transportation fee and lunch cost, due who can work at their home when who turn on their computer to enter whose employers' websites to work and make email communication to connect between them conveniently. So, I feel the online electronic book authors and online office administration jobs which will be popular further occupations to be provided from global online job structure style and many labors will like to work online, then who can raise productivity conveniently when who work at home in the future. Beside, due to online (internet) is very popular and cheap cost to be needed to spend expenditure from employer.

So, internet will build the relationships between workplaces and every staff role identity and everyday life and online working environments can connect them to work in the process of globalization in the future. Also, our everyday life and work is entering in a globalizing world. It emphasizes on time and space compression and the importance of virtual space and experience in our daily lives of many people, the working style seems spent online working time to change how our social traditional work roles and our traditional office working places-based environments to home online working environments further long time in the future. So, employers ought plan to prepare online working methods to let their employees to raise productivity.

In conclusion, Online knowledgeable job concept can raise productivity and efficiency because many office jobs can be accepted to apply online technological working in order to reduce staff numbers and to raise fast speed job efficiency as well as labors shall be prefer to work in online environment in the work.

Why does knowledgeable online jobs will raise productivity and efficiency?

Entrepreneur needs to predict when and why consumers will begin to dislike online shopping because it is possible consumers will choose any fresh or new technological consumption if it had another kind of popular technological consumption to replace online shopping. Social science can explain knowledgeable jobs will be useful and popular and assisting labors to raise productivity to work at home online working environments. It seems knowledgeable online job and undiscovered new technological consumption which will have possible close relationship and influence to any consumer's consumption of method.

Within social science, in such discipline is sociology and human psychology and geography which indicates internet technology have changed to online working place environment, sense of working place, online employee role identity, everyday online work and life style, website global working communication and email online communication working interconnections. It seems internet brings access to social, economic and political resources to effect change to both individual and social working conditions, such as employers accept to attempt to use internet to assist office staffs to work at home, e.g. many book publishing businesses like to attempt to publish electronic books from online book store, instead of book shops channel to sell paper books. So these online book stores give chance to authors to publish electronic books or online paper books from online sale channel to earn loyalty income. For example, Amazon online electronic bookstore can publish electronic books and online paper books to sell all one day 24 hours to any countries' readers from its website, so when any countries' readers can enter its website to choose any different kind of subjects of electronic books to buy by visa card conveniently. Such as fiction, psychology, economy, science, law, architecture, medicine, commerce, management etc. subjects. So, any country's reader who does not need to buy air tickets to go to the country's book shop to buy the paper book, who only needs to pay visa card to buy the electronic or online paper books from

Amazon publishing's website to buy any countries' electronic and paper books and then the overseas reader can choose either to download it from whose home computer or pays more price to deliver the online paper book to post to whose country conveniently. Hence, this online bookstore sale method will be popular and many free work authors will choose to work to raise the productivity of more quality electronic books numbers from this internet channel.

However, the consequences of global change are far from uniform with globalizing influences and adapted as new technological, economic and online working cultural experiences are incorporated by any countries' staffs of any cities, towns and rural areas into their everyday work lives from long distance easily. Since one company can employ different countries' staffs to work from internet working channel at their homes. For example, a America company can employ overseas countries' staffs to work at the same time together by sending job duties from email communication channel among them when the America company has any job arrangement to notify to any staff to finish it any time, then the overseas staff finish the job and who can send whose finished documents to whose America employer any time. It seems the overseas staffs whose working hours can be flexible and those working hours have no regular office working hours to be fixed time table, so they do not need to work in any fixed working time table every working days, who can send their finished office documents to whose employers after who have finished their documents by either email communication channel or office online website downloads office download any time conveniently.

It will be a new working style position that online working globalization is in a new stage. We are living in an age of very rapid and fluid flow of information, ideas, products and people which are having an effect of a variety of scales. I shall indicate evidences to explain why employers will be encountered online knowledgeable jobs to raise productivity in a globalizing world by sociology concept in the future one day. I shall focus on research into the connections between our everyday online life style, online working place and online working role identity.

The first is that everyday online life is the manifestation of social existence and always involves either distant or direct interaction with other people. Such as we can use internet email channel to communicate with overseas friends or strange people, even employers or employees can also use email to exchange to receive and send their office documents by email or company website any time conveniently. Good example includes such things are as online participation in work, employment, cultural events, and recreation, shopping and communication from internet channel. It is related to employees are working in whose home working places and their home working place are possible to connect their overseas employers' offices and however, readily these may be separated in far distant conceptual terms, such as an online working environment. The employee's home is such whose employer's office, who can work at home from online channel conveniently. When who receives whose employer's email about what job duties who needs to do every day. Then, who sees his employer's email, then either if who did not understand how to do whose job duties clearly, who can send email back to ask whose employers to explain how who needs to do whose office job duties by email communication channel again easily. Even after who finish whose office job duties on that day or another day, then who can send finished office job duties to whose employers by email conveniently. In this view, online working places and sense of online working places are produced by different countries' large enterprise employers and overseas employees interacting together.

At the same time, employees and employers whose sense are contacted by employees' individual role identity from email or office website communication channel any time. Thus, traditional office working environment is constrained and enabled by different countries' working histories and cultures and social class backgrounds and economic conditions and job opportunities, working positions of power and working geographical locations and development of local change and distant social interaction. In the future, online working place will be changed from traditional socially significant to online social relationship; underlying this sense of online working place will be the notion that some employers and employees themselves ought feel that life.

Moreover, online working place is the possibility of non controlling employees' working time, due to working hours are flexible and employers' working places sizes are very limited to supply to many staffs to work in a limited office working place in the same working time. It seems online home environment will be very popular, due to every employee will use whose home to work to finish whose office documents at home every day any time very conveniently as well as employers won't need to spend much expenditure to pay for large sizes of office rent when the employer needs to rent more than one room office at more than one floor in one building.

Hence, company's website expenditure can reduce the employers' office rent seriously.

Moreover, employees can be dominated by feelings towards changing general office working place to online working at home as well as changing fixed working time table to flexible working time table, e.g. the staff can see whose employer's email to know what office job duties who needs to do tonight, so who will finish whose office documents and will send whose finished office documents to whose employer by email tomorrow. So, home online working environment is seen as an ideal home working place, and home online working environment which is quiet, safe and it has certain valued facilities and home online working environment is such as the type of residents in the employee's living building. This sense of living and online work place will be held by residents who will be employed in professional/ managerial/ technical etc. occupations. Hence, local employees won't catch any transportation to go to office as well as overseas employees won't also catch planes to go to whose employer's country's office to work, due to who can use online email communication or office website communication channels to work together conveniently.

However, working facilities will be one online computer working commodity which is purchasable, useable and exchangeable and saleable to any employees are located at home and employers are located at office, and after a flexible working time table is discarded easily by employer, due to whose website or office email can receive any employee's individual finished office documents by every employee's individual email communication any time very conveniently. Moreover, home online working place is also like a stage on every employee's life is lived out. The employee will feel that whose life and working time is lived at home together at the same time. Similar to feel commodity sense of home and the working place which are the same location, but it is distinguished from it by the establishment of arriving strange and far distant of the employee's local or overseas employer's office when the employee's working place is family interacting to the employee's house or home.

Our world is entering globalization, people are connecting in an increasing number of ways. It is clear also that is the face of globalization, the ways of our everyday working life is either constituted which are still shaped by local expenditure of working place or is by where the firm's overseas employees love locally, regionally and nationally or is by the access who have limited to office resources and home office online working locations opportunity changing from general office working environment to home online working environment. Roberston (1992) shows is that" this is not just about economic processes, but about social and cultural issues are as well. In the early part of the 21 ST century, it is necessary to see this as a set of processes that encompass economic, political, social, cultural and environmental changes."

In conclusion, online knowlegeable job method can raise efficiency and productivity because many clients accept online shopping or anyundiscovered technological consumption of methods.

Why employers need to considerate labor moralty

Entrepreneurs need to consider low income level worker life challenges and how employers themselves moral behaviors to treat their employees. Because their moral behaviors will influence their employees' performance and efficiency and producticity .

Is globalization influenced to new online knowledgeable jobs to raise efficiency and productivity? One of the key areas of debate among theorists is the extent to which globalization is a new phenomenon or stage in a process. When it began and the path that it has followed and thus how new it is. Such as internet is used in communication aspect in early, e.g. hospital or war email communication channel. Then, many businessmen discovered online electronic commerce is also one online sale and purchase method. So, it will cause online office workers or online freelance online jobs, e.g. electronic book authors working style or electronic book reading cultural existed in our society in common possibly in the future.

However, I recognize globalization is a misleading concept since what is described as globalization has been happening for the 500 years history ago. Rather what is new is that human are entering an age of transition, such as online knowledgeable workers or knowledgeable nature of different jobs will be caused from online working environment popularly.

There are key processes of globalization: the economic, often is seen as the central process, the political, social, cultural and online working environment. Every natural economy needs to maintain the rate of growth, employment, welfare provision and minimum wage balance levels, so it will cause knowledgeable jobs provided, such as online organized labors, it also will change the traditional office organizational environment to cause online new organizational home work environment popularly in the future. Hence, economic and political has close connection, political and cultural has also close connection, cultural and social has also close connection, social and working environment has also connection. After all these connections cause globalization finally, then the new online knowledgeable working environment, such as online jobs will be required by global office employees popularly in the future. It will bring many online workers supply to the employment market in the future.

As capital in the new globalized economy has a limited attachment to working place, production centers, such as offices, factories or farms which locate any where it is competitively advantages to do so, and economic activity moves to where labor is cheapest or raw materials is the least expensive. It can be raised demand to online knowledgeable workers demand in global competitive employment environment directly. For example, cultural, social, global expansion of Mc Donald's and other fast food chains will be entered to the online sale channel. Hence, environmental globalization raises human awareness, includes a new view of the natural and the social worlds to environmental protection message.

These message source is from online channel popularly nowadays. Online organizing environment and living will influence our everyday working worlds. Due to many industrial cities and life will be not needed by global employers. However, industrial cities concentrate on demanding in developing countries, e.g. China, India, Korea etc. countries. So, developed countries, such as America, England, Japan etc. countries' employers will need many online knowledgeable employees to help them to work from online work place environment popular in the future. Later, knowledgeable online working environment will be popular to developing countries when which economy had developed mature in the future. So, it is possible online jobs will raise low income level householders' living of standard because online can create more job chance for this group people as well as it can bring more efficiency and productivity to employers.

Can a useful indicator measure low income living standard of labor's efficiency and performance and productivity

Nowadays, developing countries, such as India, China, Hong Kong, etc. and developed countries, such as America, England etc. which are facing social challenges. For example, many low income level labors whose income level can't be raised and inflation is also high in society. Although, these developing countries' economy is growing, but which can not raise the low income level householders' income level to let them have afford to buy one house in minimum in whose country, even these low income level family have no enough income to buy foods to eat and cloths to wear easily.

Also, the developed countries' economy had arrived the mature growing stage, but which also can not give any benefits to whose low level income level income householders group. Hence, governments have responsibilities to find methods to solve these challenges, such as: How to reduce poor occurrence? How much does economic growth help the poor? How can social policy help? Can a country have a sizeable low-wage sector of house to provide to the poor? What role can public service social spending better for the poor?

Justice is the distribution of income and wealth is fairest. Any country's government needs play a large role in determining it's citizen's abilities to do common occupation, what job choices are preferences to them, how to raise employment of motivation and what social circumstances are to cause households have no poor occurrence to cause many low level income jobs to do to earn income in society.

In order to reduce the unfair income distribution between rich and poor people. Why it is important to improve unfair income treatment between rich and poor people to any countries? However, in a rich and growing economic country, such as America, England etc. , which are difficult to justify stagnant living standards for those at the floor bottom low income people nowadays. Although, these developed countries' economy are growing, but which can not give benefits to this low level income households group.

However, I suggest any country ought favor not simply a satisfactory level of living standards for the poor people, but it ought consider how to improve or review poor people living standards every year. Analysts typically set the poverty line at 50 or 60 percent of the median income within each country. In general, poverty means to level of resources insufficient to achieve a minimal acceptable standard of living as well as people tends to experience poverty as relative is to living standards by comparison in any country's citizen's own society. If the absolute incomes or living standards for the poor grow less rapidly than those of households in the middle income level in the country. So, it seems that it is not fair economic growth in these developing countries and income seems to be a useful indicator to measure living of standard.

How to apply " standard growth enhancing policy" to
improve low income level householders living of
standard to raise productivity

Is income a useful indicator of living standards? Income is a resource that allows any country's households to acquire the sort of things e.g. food, housing, medical care, transportation, education, entertainment etc. needs. So, which are needed for a minimal decent standard of living. Income also is comparatively easy to measure. However, causing poor factors might have many reasons, such as illness, temporary unemployment, a large amount of bonus reduction, overtime long time working hours, family members unemployment, even economic decline (falling down), so these factors can reduce jobs supply to any countries to cause poor occurrence.

However, any countries' income measures seldom include the value of government service and in kind benefit, such as pension, unemployment assistance etc. as well as some low income households have assets (savings in bank, and owned home). So, it seems income is not an accurate measure to the actual living standard to the low income people numbers in the countries effectively. If income is not an accurate measure to actual living standard, then it can not improve the low income level householders of living standard and productivity level will be reduced because these low income level labors can not get reasonable salaries and unfair welfare to work from whose employers. Otherwise, the high income level labors can get increased salaries and fair welfare to work from whose employers. When these both low and high income level labors work in same company, the low income level labors will feel angry to work unhappy, then it is possible that who will decrease their productivity.

The poor people numbers will be reduced possibly. How to evaluate the actual poor people numbers decreasing? In think when the degree to the country which economic growth boosts the income level of low and households to rise their general savings amounts to the income level of middle households. Then, the country's poor people numbers will be decreasing, due to this group of the numbers of incomes level of low households has been decreasing and it's numbers has been increasing to the income level of middle group, then productivity will also raise to every employers in any country.

In general, economic growth is assumed that poor households get more jobs, work more hours and/or receives higher wages. Hence, when one country measure economic growth, which can apply the relationship between per capita GDP and low income households of numbers between the past year and current year to measure the rising or falling numbers per capita GDP in the low and income households group, for example, in

Sweden, Denmark, Norway, the Netherlands and Finland countries which net transfers are received by low income level households increased significantly between 1979 year and 2007 year. But, average earnings, were flat in Demarks country, when in Sweden and Finland countries which declined sharply during those countries' deep recessions in the early 1990 year. Otherwise, in the United Kingdom, the period was from 1979 year to 1995 year, it saw no changes in transfers pension or retirement savings from United Kingdom government and a slight drop in earnings, but from 1999 year to 2005 year, social earning increased slightly, but more important was a large rise in net government pension and retirement saving transfers, which resulted in a sizeable increase in low income level incomes group. When net government pension or retirement savings transfers to citizen increased this was caused by economic growth. In general, economic growth allows policy makers to boost inflation-adjusted benefit levels for pension or retirement saving transfer to citizen programs, which will increased the incomes of pension or retirement saving benefit recipients. With GDP rising, government social benefit pension or retirement saving transfers as a share of GDP tended to remark more or less constant.

However, in some countries, the rise in pension of retirement saving net transfers was achieved in part by reduction of income or profit taxes for low income households or low business profit households, since the 1970 year, most of the world's rich nations, such as America, united Kingdom have not significantly increased the share of their GDP that goes to pensions or retirement savings transfer for the low income level poor households. It seems that if any country hoped the low income level of householders numbers will be increase, which ought need to upgrade their low income level to go up middle income level in society, then its economic growth will be raising. How economic growth can boost incomes for the poor households. It seems economic growth has made rising low income level of households is more likely, but several countries are exceptions. They experienced growing per capita GDP, but little or no improvement in the income of low income level of households, such as Hong Kong has seven million people who are living in a small city.

Although, it was encountering economic growth from 1970 year in beginning, but the low income level of households had little or no improvement, it was possible that the numbers of Hong Kong low income level of households are more than the middle or high income level of households seriously. So, the HK economic growth seems not improve low income level of households to assist this low income level of households to raise whose income to be risen to the middle income level of households group. The reason is possible that the failure of some governments to increase public transfers as the economy grows is a key part of reason. But why did not more economic growth reach the low income level of poor households in the form of rising market income? For example, in HK, whether economic growth is likely to directly benefit the poor group's employment hours reduction and rising hourly wage levels. However, I discovered that HK economic growth produced no increase in the wage or salary market rate of low level of income households and without employment hours reduction and without rising hourly wage levels. So, HK economic growth seems to raise more job supply in the employment market, but it seems without employment hours reduction. Otherwise, it's economic growth rises employment hours, but without rising hourly wage. Hence, it seems low income level householders of numbers and economic growth have close relationship to any country, so employers need to concern their labors numbers of low income level to raise their income to be middle income level in society.

Why economists need to concern ethic to raise productivity

Entrepreneur needs to concern business ethic to whose employees because employees' negative emotion will influence whose performance and productivity to be poor. I recommend this economic policy to reduce poor occurrence, such as growth on average benefit the poor as much as anyone lives in the country's society, such as "standard growth enhancing policy" should be at the center of any poverty reduction strategy. I believe economic growth is the most powerful instrument for reducing poverty, due to many businessmen have enough money to invest to their countries to do any kind of businesses, then the jobs supply will be raised any many people can get any jobs supply number is more than job seekers number, then it is no doubt, the unemployment numbers will be reduced. When many people have new jobs to do and who can earn enough wages to prepare to save more money in bank.

What has been the impact of economic growth on employment hours and wages? In fact, work hours are matter a great deal for the incomes of poor group of households in developed countries, such as United States or United Kingdom or developing countries, such as Hong Kong, China etc. countries.

For example, HK economic growth has a large influence to raise employment hours more than rising wage levels, such as HK general working hours are risen up to 10 to 12 hours or more per week working days to low income level of households, but the low income level of households group has not been rising wage level generally. So, I feel HK economic growth could not give any benefits to the low income level of households, such as without reduction employment hours and without raising wage level to the low income level of households in HK. Also, HK's economic growth only raises many jobs supply in HK society. Otherwise, America economic growth can give benefits to low income level of households, such as reduction employment hours, rising wage level to low income level of households and raising jobs supply in America society. Hence, the developed countries, such as America , England which economic growth can give more benefits to low income level of households. Otherwise, the developing countries, such as India, China, Korea which economic growth can not give more benefits to the low income level of households and these developing countries will cause disadvantages to this low income level of poor group in society. It is possible that the developing countries' low income level of households often need to increase to spend more working hours to assist whose employers to develop whose employers' business, due to their employers do not want to increase to employ extra workers or staffs to assist whose business development, who need whose current employees to raise more extra working hours to work to raise work efficiency when these developing countries are encountering the economic growth stage.

For example, HK employers do not concern moral issues about abnormal working hours influence. The outcome is either Hong Kong labors work long time working hours abnormally who can not rise Hong Kong economic growth or who can rise Hong Kong economic growth in long time. Generally, Hong Kong employers choose to pay less salary expenditure to need many extra labors to work abnormal working hours to help them to rise productivity, but who don't concern that long time working factor will influence unhealthy to current workers due to who need to work long time working hours abnormally in long time and it seems to cause their workers will reduce productivity and inefficiency in long time.

Although, it is possible that HK labors can be increased extra abnormal working hours to work to rise Hong Kong employers' productivity and assist HK social economy will be grown up in short term, but it is also possible that it can't rise Hong Kong economic growth due to their unhealthy or sick increasing to cause productivity declining and inefficiency in long time. Thus, I shall find evidence to analyze whether Hong Kong labors need to work abnormal long time working hours. Otherwise, who will decline Hong Kong economic growth and reduce productivity and inefficiency in long time as well as I shall give suggestion to indicate whether either current workers work abnormal long time working hours or employers ought choose to employ more extra part time workers to assist current labors to rise their productivity to decide which is the best choice to raise HK economic growth and efficient productivity in long time.

Effects on Hong Kong employment of working time reduction is found to be difficult to predict. The results of Hong Kong macroeconomic simulations of the effects on employments of working time reduction rely heavily on certain basic assumptions, such as how many hours people will actually work or how productivity and pay levels will develop. Whether HK abnormal working hours will assist HK social economic growth or economic falling down in long term.

The reasons cause Hong Kong labors who need to work abnormal long time working hours. In fact, it isn't the reason that the Hong Kong high skillful labors market is shortage to supply for the nature of some occupations, e.g. hospital doctors and nurses, university teachers, law firm lawyers etc. professional occupations. HK has many high qualification university students graduation, it has enough labor supply to high labor market every year. The reason is that employers don't like to spend more salary to increase to employ extra labors to share current workers workload, such as low skillful and hardworking labors, such as cleaners, securities, waiters and high skillful professionals, such as hospital doctors and nurses, university teachers, lawyers etc. However, the low and high skillful labor market can be enough supply in Hong Kong, but Hong Kong employers need the current high and low both skillful workers who need to work more than 10 to 12 hours or more per working day commonly. It is possible that HK high and low educational labors will be caused unhealthy and lack enough sleep if who still need to work abnormal working hours time in long time. Although, who can rise productivity and efficiency in the short time, but it is possible that who can't rise productivity and inefficiency in the long time. Moreover, it will cause many young or middle or old ages high educational or low educational knowledgeable hardworking workers who will lose many jobs provided and who will be hard to find any jobs in HK labor employment market if HK employers don't choose to pay extra salaries to employ extra full time workers to share current labors' workload in the high and low salary occupations, due to they only choose to increase abnormal additional extra working hours to current workers to achieve to reduce employment expenditure and raise productivity. Hence, it is possible to influence HK social economy grows up slowly, even it's economy can go down seriously in long time.

I shall assume that working wage or salary of every individual labors can not be increased, even can be decreased as well as whose normal working hours can be increased abnormally in generally. This means that the Hong Kong individual worker's income will be decreased and general productivity raising is not affected generally, due to HK employers need current labors to work abnormal extra working hours to attempt to raise productivity daily, but their salary or wage have not increased more. However, HK employers need many workers to accomplish the same amount of work, even who don't like to employ extra labors to assist current workers to achieve long term productivity raising in their companies. These abnormal working hours labors will feel unfair treatment, due to they need to work abnormal working hours, but their salary or wage have not been increased.

In the first scenario of my hypothesis is about that HK labor employment market's general salary or wage has not been increased to the normal proportion of the increased extra abnormal working time(hours). Then, in HK labors market, due to the numbers of labors supply is more than the jobs supply because HK employers don't like to pay more salary or wage expenditure to employ extra labor, but they like to increase extra abnormal working hours to current workers to aim to achieve productivity. So it will cause many HK job seekers with adequate qualifications or with less qualifications who won't find any jobs easily, then the HK the numbers of unemployed people will be increased and their household incomes will decrease to cause many HK household do not like to spend easily. The result will cause a negative effect on HK social private consumption will be decreased and the businessmen' income will be decreased also. So, HK people private consumption decreasing will influence HK economy growth to be slow, even it will cause HK economy declining in the long time.

In the second scenario of my hypothesis is about that Hong Kong workers are fully compensated for the increasing extra abnormal working time(hours) by the abnormal additional working hours calculation. Although, Hong Kong companies' productivity will be raised, but which are not to the extent that it compensates Hong Kong enterprises for their increased wage or salary costs. In fact, Hong Kong enterprises, their costs are passed on to the clients, it causes Hong Kong's economic growth has an impact on international competitiveness to cause economic declining in possible when these enterprises need to raise their products' sale prices to balance their salary or wage cost raising to win their import competitors. Another effect is that Hong Kong individual labor's incomes decrease, which means that Hong Kong private consumption also falls in this scenario to influence HK economic growth seriously. Thus, the HK economic growth problem will be caused, due to these factors lead to a fall in Hong Kong social household private consumption. Consequently, it will cause many HK employers hope to raise Hong Kong productivity and they will raise the total amount of Hong Kong labor actually worked hours will be risen to such as extent as the increasing in normal working time(hours) from 8 or 9 hours per normal working day to 10 or 11 or 12 hours, even more extra abnormal hours per working day to the current labors. But they do not like to spend more salary or wage expenditure to employ full time extra labors, instead of increasing extra abnormal working hours to current labors to achieve productivity of raising, due to the cost will be increased if they choose to employ extra full time labors if they want to raise productivity. However, I feel they will raise productivity in the short term, but they will not raise productivity in the long term when they choose to raise their current labors abnormal working hours per working day.

The assumption will be made regarding to the relationship between the HK labor market's abnormal long time working hours factor and whether it can influence Hong Kong economic growth in long time for this research economic problem. For example, how many hours Hong Kong labor would actually work or how much workers have efficient productivity and efficiency and how much salaries or wages would be affected as a result of the increasing in working time(hours) in Hong Kong employment market.

I shall apply endogenous growth theory to Hong Kong labor market. As this theory indicates that this model also incorporated a new concept of human capital, whose capital is increasing rates of return. Research done in this area has focused on what increases human capital (e.g. education) or technological change (e.g. innovation) to influence HK economic growth. In macro economic environment, it indicates that economic growth means the increase in the market value of the products and services produced by the country's economy over time. It is conventionally measured as the percent rate of increase in real growth domestic product or real GDP. The growth of the ratio of GDP to population (GDP per capital, per capita income). Thus, an increase in growth is caused by more efficient use of inputs is referred to as intensive growth. GDP growth is caused only be increased in such as capital, population or territory is called extensive growth. Thus, in economy growth theory, typically refers growth off potential output, i.e. production is at full employment. However, HK unemployment ratio is still high to compare other developed or developing countries, although the labors supply are enough to HK employment market.

The working time is the period of time that an individual spends at paid occupation labor. Many countries regulate the work week by law, such as minimum daily rest periods, annual holidays and a maximum number of working hours per week. Working time may vary from person to person often depending on location, cultural, lifestyle choice and the profitability of the individual's livelihood.

Generally, most Hong Kong employers need labors work long time working hours abnormally. For example, low educational workers, such as security occupations of labors need to work per working day is twelve hours or more, restaurant waiters and dish cleaners also need to work ten to twelve hours or more per working day, bank counter cashiers or audit firm staffs also need to work over time from 10 to 12 hours or more per working day and who have no extra salaries for over time salaries payment commonly. Standard working hours or normal working hours refers to the legislation to limit the working hours per day, per week, per month or per year. If an employee needs to work overtime, the employer will need to pay overtime payments to employees as required in the law. Generally speaking, standard working hours countries word wide are around 40 to 44 hours per week (but not everywhere: such as France employers need labors work from 35 hours per week, North Korea employers need labors work up to 112 hours per week). Maximum working hours refers that the employee can't work than the level specified in the maximum working hours law. It seems that Hong Kong many employers had needed labors to work above standard working hours per week to compare to other developed countries, e.g. America, France, England, New Zealand etc. developed countries.

In conclusion, in my viewpoint, HK employers need to provide on job training to current labors to aim to raise their efficiency to productivity in the long time. Because when their labors had been trained to let them to learn how to use special skill to finish their job duties easily, then they will not need to spend much time (additional working hours) to finish their job duties per working day. On the one hand, HK employers need to measure to compare what benefits are in favor of standard working hours to whose employees. The benefits include, such as promoting work life balance and enjoy family life, increasing time for leisure and rest, beneficial to health and employees can have more time to pursue further studies as well as employers do not need to pay higher salaries to longer working hours employees or overtime pay boost income as most HK companies pay time and a half to some employees only. On the other hand, HK employers need to measure to compare what benefits are against standard working hours to employers, such as employing many part time working hours employees to assist normal working hours full time employees rather than needing full time employees work abnormal hours daily, lowering or cancelling year and bonus etc. Moreover, HK employers may also use various measure to offset the increased cost of running businesses, such as lowering average hourly annual compensation. However, when HK employees are forced to work part time jobs, who may need to acquire additional employment to maintain their standard living. Even, HK employers only force employees to work overtime in some situations. Appropriate standard working hours can vary across different industries based on the type of work performed. Such as some HK certain professional positions are difficult to define in terms of appropriate working hours. Issues can arise with employers expecting employees to work extra hours "off the clock" in order to keep costs down. Thus, I believe that HK labors abnormal working hours time issue ought be decreased and HK employers ought employ extra workers assistance to share current labors' workload to help them to raise productivity and efficiency and HK economy will grow fast in the long time. Finally, my research aims to find that the number of hours worked is a more responsive measure of the state of the labor market than employment in HK. Comparing the number of hours worked to indicators of the wider economy shows that it is likely to be demand from HK firms (employers) which is driving the numbers of hours, rather than individual job applicant supply to HK employment market. My analysis also show that the HK appears to have developed a long working hours culture to compare other developed countries, such as America, England, Canada etc. In fact, in the presence of HK firms may even invest to find which are more profitable to able to reduce their every employee's abnormal working hours daily rather than normal number of working hours of their every employee.

Finally, I shall recommend some methods to rise the living standard to low income level households group in any countries. On the income policy, I recommend governments ought implement the progressive tax policy, so the income taxes tend to be progressive to the middle and high income level of households. It aims to achieve the low income level group and the middle and high income level groups whose income level to be balanced. Whereas taxes on payroll and consumption usually are regressive, due to payroll and consumption taxes are more useful than income taxes for increasing revenues taxes on income and payroll are the least conductive to economic growth, so payroll taxes can raise growth of employment in possible. Because the low income level of households have no more effort to spend to buy any expensive products or foods generally, so who can pay less taxes when who spend less. Otherwise, because the middle or high income levels of households have more effort to spend to buy any expensive products or foods generally, so who need pay more taxes when who spend more. It is possible to reduce the level amount of difference of savings between the low income level of households and the middle income level of households. Finally, I conclude that the method of taxes on payroll and consumption usually are regressive and the method of income taxes tend to be progressive to the middle and high income level of households, which are possible to raise the low income level of households of living standard for long term if governments could attempt to achieve these two policies to apply to the low income level group and the middle income level groups both, such as income tax and payroll or consumption tax policies both. It aims to raise the better of standard of life to the low income level household and to assist the low income level household can be upgrade to the middle income level household group in the short time quickly.

Economists claim to be scientists or technicians who study fact, not values, who make scientific studies and predictions to decide why this matter is caused and to find the reasons. Often the public sector economists in USA predict the economic processes and find the facts of the world have not supported the economists' models wrongly. However, economists have ethical rules to control their behaviors to be judged any matter and to give the corrective and reasonable decisions to let public to know correctively. Hence, who can't attempt to mislead facts to present to let public to receive the wrongly message to achieve themselves unreasonable benefits and rewards. In fact, economist is similar to lawyer or accountant profession, who need to provide a "service" discipline to give corrective and reasonable judgement and facts and who can not attempt to mislead to publish whose economic research reports to let public to get wrong information frequently. I believe that the scientific of economics of the 20ᵗʰ century fully accepts the ethical separation. Economic theory is seen as a positive science which has to analyze and to explain the mechanisms of economic processes. Ethical valuations should not form part of the economist's research program. Modern economics stresses rational calculation, the base material objections and scientific neutrality on moral issues. I think whose idea is concerned micro economy is based on assumptions of rationally selfish behavior.

Whether what is concerned to current ethical crisis in economics? Economic matters have been debated throughout human history. I feel economic ethical matters which can be concerned in aspects, such as wealth accumulation, lending, business and commerce economic issues, journals or reports or books publishing. Due to any economic matters happen in economic processes which will be recorded in history, then economists will analyze why these issues are caused and find what reasons which cause the economic issue happening is discussed by theology, ethics and politics issues are as view points. So, the moral and ethics is needed to concern to any economists when who need to do any economic research nowadays.

Economy is concerned to human will face limited resources to use or spend, so economy theory indicates to be researched what methods how human chooses to allocate resources to achieve the efficient and effective result. Economy aims to achieve human rationality to control the desire to acquire material products in order to allow better satisfaction of the true human need. Many economists concern for others now directly affects one's own welfare and commitment drives between personal choice and personal welfare and thus undermines modern economics ethic. Individuals frequently display commitment, acting against their own welfare in favor of the group. This element of ethical behavior has been ignored by economists and needs to be brought into the analysis. Although ethical motivation are relevant to economists, but the capabilities approach is more concerned with social achievement. To a large degree, this is a theory of distributive justice that economy and political science and philosophy theories which have more relationship among of these three subjects theories.

Why ethic relates to labor behavior

Entrepreneur needs to considers ethic issue can influence labor behavior indirectly. I shall give some current economists' judgement to indicate how well human are doing according to the capability standard to prove why employers need to concern moral behavior. The capability approaching requires that many means be provided to every person. This is an alternative to social achievement from economics approach, which uses the quantity of commodities available for consumption. The conventional measure of the standard of living (GDP/head) has been subject to sustained criticism in recent times, one source of the complaints is the capability theorists.

This capabilities approach is a new inter-disciplinary social science and there are still many problems with this approach to concern ethical issues of mainstream economics. However, some economists feel that ethical motivations exist and play a role in human's actual behavior. Human well being refers to living a full human life. It measures to show the things that demonstrate a good life being lived. So, human functioning achievements, must be the focus. Possession of a certain quantity of commodities, however, may be necessary in order to achieve human functioning. This provides social success in delivering well being across our society. Moreover, some scientists who also believe the standard of social success may be limited to basic functioning. Alternatively, a rich of human group may be accepted, but social success may be considered for only a small proportion of the population. So, for each theorist, we need to ask these following questions. Does the theorist present an ethical view of motivation? Does the theorist adopt a deep mind of human well being? In the assessment of social success, does the theorist concern human functioning achievements and means to promote functioning achievements?

I shall analyze on individual psychology, household psychology and social achievement three aspects to indicate labor morality and raising productivity and even economic growth has close relationship as below:

In economic view, household means a family which has female control functioning. On the individual and public policy means that support individual achievements. However, in concept analysis, I shall indicate three levels of analysis to economic ethic of human behavior. The lowest level is individual, it is individual psychology, human functioning and ethical motivation. The middle level is household, it is household management, moral education, character formation. The highest level is the city, it is social achievement (Public policy supports equipment needs for individual capability achievement and formative law). So, human's behavioral is an assumption of modern economics. From history viewpoint, our economic conditions are largely agricultural with some mining, manufacturing and commerce, there was limited scope for domestic and international markets;

mutual give and take, lending and borrowing between households was widespread. Commonly, these activities are general human economic behavior of reasons to cause these business activities in our society.

Firstly, on individual psychology aspect, human's economy of behavior is in our society, human needs do this economy behavior because human needs have good life and education, the good life required leisure and the good use of leisure time to do leisure activities with friends. Otherwise, leisure required freedom from the duties of earning a living. It was commonly accepted that the good life is required to work to earn, such as labors, traders, professions, farmers etc. service or labor occupations their individual behavior is aim to achieve earning for good life and education. So, who need to spend some time to do economic activities to aim to earn some time for leisure and education.

Secondly, on household management psychology aspect, in general, managing revenues and expenditures is a part of household management. However, household management requires moderation on the desires for food, wine, sex and sleep. So, in labor economy relationship, household seems to be the frame of mind and habits needed for engineering to make sense. In old age, expenditure on subsistence continues, but no one will pay for the labor of the old. Saving for old age, therefore is sensible. However, if one is habituated in youth to lazy, one will find it hand to change later. Nevertheless, these habits are unsustainable in old age, when one can't be labor and generate income. Hence, in labor economy view, moderation is an essential element of good household management. Although, wealth is also important, but more important is the knowledge or skill of household management. However, if one has no leisure and is unable to develop his capabilities (including bodily and non-bodily pleasures to easy to live with). Then, productivity will be reduce and inefficient work, due to the labor is hard to work, who feel himself/herself is such as a machine and who has no much time to rest often. Also the earning of friendship is also important, including certain market relationships in our modern societies. Clearly human's labor economy of behavior of household management in the broad sense is a comprehensive act and part of a way of human life. Hence, an ethical understanding is also needed, such as friendship relationship to complete household management in the middle level of household management between the city level and individual level. On functioning achievement and freedom to individual of labor economy behavior, it includes education, increased physical training etc. economic benefits to our individual in our society. Just as the city is a complex structure, so is human psychology to cause labor economy behavior. Justice in the city is defined as each class (and each individual within the class) doing its own job, justice in the individual is defined as each part of individual doing its own job. Hence, a good city has all of the individuals correctly assigned to the different classes and each individual and each class performs its appropriate job. Similarly, the good individual has each of labor's performing its job appropriately.

In the final social achievement aspect, it concerns micro. As the growth of the healthy city showed up to a certain point, economic development is required in terms of the city's physical size and population. So, modern economic principles are adopted (such as economic development and the division of labor). Nevertheless, our society must be justify to some degree to market relations. Various property rights and exchange justice must be enforced. These principles, however are limited by other ethical principles guiding the laws. Nevertheless, citizens are to be banned from engaging in most occupations. For example, the moral dangers of commercial activities are great. Moreover, market are limited to a specific location and regulated by market regulators. Although, duties are not imposed on foreign trade, prohibitions apply to various unnecessary imports and to exports of necessities. Hence, it will influence labor demand and job supply to influence the country's economic development in any time. To analyze labor economy, we need to know human nature and to establish the functions of human beings. These functions are shared with human beings, e.g. humans need to eat, drink. As a general rule, the passions that drive human to satisfy these needs, but it is of limited amount to supply.

So, these factors will influence labor's behavior between action, motivation and character. However, every organization is influenced to economic growth every year by its staff individual behavior, such as its staff individual has passions and emotions disposed toward bad action and decides to act well for other reasons, e.g. the staff feels fear of detection or punishment and then who will act well because of the staff's self control to avoid the firm will dismiss him/her in the firm. It seems the staff's passion, emotion will influence whose behavior to be good or bad to do whose work in whose firm. Hence, the firm needs have economic analysis to decide to dismiss the staff or not dismiss the staff if it discovered whose behavior is not acceptable to its firm and what it will be influenced from whose bad behavior in the short term and long term. If the staff is very important and if who left this firm, this firm will face business failure challenge because it has no any right applicant or another staff who can do this staff's job easily. Hence, in labor economy analysis, the firm needs to judge the benefits are much or the losses are much before which decide to dismiss the staff.

What are ethics? Ethics are a set of values or group of moral principles that are right and good a code or principles of behavior or conduct governing an individual or group. For example, when a engineer needs to do any researching jobs which concern to engineering, who needs to increase whose ability as engineer to responsibly confront moral issues raised by technological activity, not always in short term best interest, and long term into decision making ethics are imprecise, complex, and in a given situation may conflict. Who will have these questions to concern before who does his duties, such as does it pass the benefits /harm test? Whom does it harm? Whom does it benefit? Can these be justified, cost/ benefit analysis risk assessment? Does it treat everyone equally? equitable? If not, can the differences be justified? However, any employer needs to concern whose labor ethics issues, who have four aspects need to be considered, such as:

On the first concerning aspect, it is working condition ethics, whether the employer's act is moral right when it respects right relevant to a work environment or employment condition of situation. For example, whether the employer can provide whose employees have rights for life, liberty, pursuit of happiness, human rights and non-human rights, e.g. clean and safe working environment or fair salary and welfare, unreasonable normal working hours. On the second concerning aspect, it is duty ethics, whether the employer acts it is right when it conforms with ethics duties to whose employees, e.g. uphold promise, be fair treatment to job nature and duty, respect personal freedom, duty to protect the weak, duty to comply with employment laws, duty to do job to best of ability. On the third concerning aspect, it is utilitarianism ethic, whether the employer has right action consists in producing good consequences to whose employees, e.g. good intentions, outcomes, honesty, fairness, conscientiousness etc. On the final concerning aspect, it is the situational ethics, which means that depending on the specific circumstance, different rights, duties, values, etc. the right circumstance may be applied to whose labors, e.g. whether the workers work in the dirty and dark factory and who need to work abnormal working hours. It seems that if the working environment is not suitable to the employees to feel to work, it will influence the labors raise to work inefficient and poor performance.

So, employers need to concern their ethics to labor, it include moral development to labor, which are often classified such as, obedience or punishment, marketplace morality, conformity, law and order, social contract, universal human rights and integrity whole environment ethic moral development of issues. However, emotion is one important factor to influence labor's individual performance and productivity and efficiency to any employer. How emotional labor and ethic of care will influence productivity. Employers concern care which ought be more than labor itself. Labor's activity that is fundamentally about maintaining, continuing and repairing the working economic world, so that labor can live in it as well as possible. An ethic of labor care is more than a list of moral principles, the ethic of care labor elements, it includes attentiveness, responsibility, competence and responsiveness.

However, employers need to make distinctions between " caring for" and "caring about" to labor ethic. "Caring about" is directed toward less concrete objects/subjects. It is a general form of commitment to employees, when "caring for" focuses on a specific object/subject and responds to the particular, physical, spiritual, intellectual and emotional needs of labor. Caring labor is too inclusive of all kinds of economic activities. So employers ought not care relations too narrowly, but should include care is given by extended to employees' families, such as domestic workers and workers in hospitals and teachers etc. service labor occupations. So, labor care ethic relates to the work that employers do under the working conditions within which the employers' labor. Also, a labor care ethic is a deeply relational framework involving both labor care activities and practices as well as a habit of labor care mind. So, employers ought presume that dependent is valued, accepted and universal, it necessitates that care labor to every is shared equally and the society policy also needs to be promoted care labor values to let employers to concern this care labor issue. Care ethic means that empathy and responsiveness, among others, coming out of practices and experiences of " doing care". However, the important aspects of a care ethic that complicates our understanding of the reproduction of alienated labor under capitalism as well as in carrying out care labor, caring for the recipient is an expected part of that work.

In labour ethic view, employers ought attempt to answer this question. Does the expectation of such affective emotions necessitate a different formulation of compensation? In examining the relationship between an ethic of care and the alienation under capitalist relations of production.

For example: What does make a "good work" ? Is a good worker someone who cares about whose work? How much should the worker care for the recipient of the labour? What does about the customer service representative who care about assisting someone? or does the retail salesperson care about helping someone look good? or does the carpenter care for the wood with which he is working? Whether the worker may or may not take time, be attentive, responsive and responsible. So, I suggest "caring about" and "caring for" the work and the recipient implies a relational experience with others. Many workers care about the outcome of their labour, whether a final product or service. They take pride in their work, they care about doing a good job, they take care of the people with whom who encounter in the process. In this way, workers make their work meaningful, who attempt to connect to it and to those who are "served" when carrying out the work.

Nowadays, human are encountering of an expended service economy, care and the emotional labour involved in such work. For example, luxury hotel workers are interactive service workers both consented to activity investing in the work, also luxury service is not only about what workers do; it is also about how they do it. Luxury service means that how workers make their jobs meaningful, become invested in them, and construct images of themselves as skilled and autonomous. For example, flight attendants who are the caring and emotional labour that is expected of these workers and it is the caring for the recipient, which allows workers to find meaning, creativity and feel connected to the work itself. I also think that labouring makes "real" something outside of the individual, the commodity as value is imposed external to the thing and to the labour itself. Under conditions of private property, the worker is disconnected from whose own creative powers and the objects of the labour become alien to the worker. So, I think employers ought not take away any labour whose individual's specific life, e.g. For long term abnormal working hours will reduce any labour's leisure and family private time.

However, I think labour can divide two kinds of physical labour and emotional labour. For example, the a factory worker works from whose own body and so who is a physical labour. Otherwise, a flight attendant works from whose own feelings and so who is a emotional labour. However, for the particular features of service -oriented labour, who needs to take "caring for" someone is central, necessarily alter these survival techniques. In care work, it is the consumers/recipients of care who expect that those who do caring work care about the work who do and care for the recipients of their care labour, e.g. hotel employees need to shoe genuine care and concern for guests' needs. So, care is the expected and central element of the labour and I think that health attendants and nurses home health carers etc. service workers who need provide more emotional service to whose clients, so who belong to emotional service labour seriously. For example, nursing profession, nurses are thought about as caring, moral creatures who show kindness and comfort to their patients. It is the doctors who are assumed to possess skills and knowledge. How care labour may be negatively affected, such as underpaid, overworked may happen in a situation where the care-giver is compensated unjustly and treated unfairly. Is it possible to argue that if care labour or any labour carried out in the context of a care ethic, the work that is done could be so much better for the whole of society and for the person doing the work and recipients of the work? In an ethic of care that predominates, would we simply value the labour of chid-care workers or home care attendants etc. workers? Would we reflect better compensation, better treatment and better working conditions because our relationship with ourselves and each other are acknowledged and values?

Hence, care activities are needed to focus on caring labour, e.g. nurses, personal attendants or home care workers and child care workers. That is, assuming the existence of a care ethic, such questions must be applied to any and all work activities that we do. Does every economic activity contain caring practices, even traditionally non care labour? I think caring about what we do and how we do it, we may help to improve our relations with others, thus reflecting an ethic of care. Does caring labour help to make invisible, reduce its harm to the self and society? It may be true that workers cared for their work, product or service, this would serve the needs of the employers quite well. How do we care for/about something but against the exploitation produced by capital labour relations? Is it good for society as a whole to care about what you do, care for the work you do, Does the product you make or the service you provide even if it enriches the owner and exploits the worker? What about the office cleaner who cleans the office effectively and efficiently in order to keep whose job that who desperately needs. Should the office cleaner care about doing a good job, care for the faceless people who doesn't know?

A care ethic both encourages this type of work ethic and at the same time, these relations are created and who serve are expected to care for and about the recipients of care, the customer is always right. However, structural inequalities between consumers and workers are normalized in the process. For the nurses and home care workers, the work becomes their own, who become attached to the work, connected to the process and the final outcome, and the work gives meaning to their live. At the same time, when workers don't care about whose work, when they don't care for their charges, or for the service who are offering. Should it, when may the labour be a child care provider neglecting the needs of the child? Or of the overworked social worker dismissing the needs of whose client in order to fill paperwork that who is directed to complete. Hence, I recommend employers need to concern about care is needed such as a practice, value, ethic activity to their labours. The elements of care, its affective emotional and relational qualities help to give meaning to the work for the worker. At the same time, it could be an ethic of care, where individuals view themselves as relational, identifying our connections to others and mutual responsibilities for each other become the necessary conditions for a working class politics.

Labour market equilibrium is an important issue to be concerned in law economy and ethic aspect. Workers prefer to work when the wage is high, and firms prefer to hire when the wage is low generally. Labour market equilibrium "balance out" the conflicting desires of workers and firms and determines the wage and employment observed in the labour market. If labour markets are competitive and if firms and workers are free to enter and leave; the equilibrium allocation of workers to firms is efficient; the sorting of workers and firms are accumulated by trading each other. In fact, labour markets are efficient plays a role by the public policy. Many government programs are often debated whether the particular policy leads to a more efficient allocation of resources or whether the efficiency costs are substantial.

Labour market equilibrium occurs when labour supply equals labour demand, generating the competitive wage(w) and employment (E). The wage (w) is the market clearing wage because any other wage level would create either upward or downward pressures on the wage. It would be too many jobs to supply, but the few available workers or too many workers competing for the few available job determined. Due to the competitive wage level is determined in this industry fashion, each firm in the industry hires workers up to the point where the value of marginal product of labour equals the competitive wage. Then, it seems the industry worker's wage level has arrived the maximum labour market wage level. So, employers ought not need to increase whose wage to attract more workers to choose to do whose industry often because it is not reasonable wage level increasing when the labour supply number is enough at the moment. Also the labour market of the industry has implied it's worker demand numbers has arrived the equal level of job supply numbers in the stage. What is caused to happen by worker surplus? When the difference between what the worker receives, that is the competitive wage(w) and the value of the worker's time outside the labour market gives the gains to workers. So, it will cause the excess workers have a value of marginal product that is less than their value of time. In effect, those workers are not being efficiently used by the labour market. So, firms ought to learn how to allocate the right number of persons to different positions that maximizes the total gains and firms ought need to learn how to form trade in the labour market in any efficient allocation way. Search of labour economy, the central aim is to examine how a work perspective, countries can develop their skills base to increase both the quantity and the productivity of labour employed in the country. Inadequate education and skills of labour development can influence any countries' overall economic development in long term. So, governments need to achieve good policies to solve this issue. Due to skills and education development is central to improve productivity. Because productivity is an important source of improved living standards and growth. Other critical factors include macroeconomic policies maximize opportunities for poor employment growth, an enabling environment is for enterprise development and fundamental investments in education, health and physical to income level households. So, effective skills development systems which is needed to connect education to technical training, technical training to labour market entry and labour market entry to workplace to long life learning to concentrate on providing to low income level households.

Productivity growth can reduce production costs and increase returns on investments. Some of which provide greater income for business owners which some are given higher wages to labours. However, the productivity of individuals may be reflected in employment rates, wage rates, stability of employment, job satisfaction or employability across jobs or industries. The productivity of enterprises, in addition to output per worker may measure in terms of market share and export performance. The benefits to societies from higher individual and enterprise productivity may be evident in increased competitiveness and employment or in a shift of employment from low to higher productivity sector. So, employers can use this method to measure every employee's morality and job behaviour performance to judge whether their job ethic and job attitude whether which can adopt to continue to work in whose organizational environment. If the employer discovered the employee's morality and job behaviour performance and job attitude is not achieved to whose work performance standard, then who can decide to either reduce whose salary or dismiss him/her or not increasing whose salary for long term any decision. So, labour ethic issue is very important to influence economic growth to any countries.

Whether labour ethic has close relationship to economic growth. I feel this issues concerns any stage of the labour life cycle and organization life cycles, it includes the link between the design of economic theory and labour individual morality and job behaviour and performance. In fact, we need to suppose all research questions and labour economy is as mapping to particular stages of an individual's life cycle to labour economy ought be related to the accumulation of human (labour) capital, labour market entry and labour supply choices, behaviour within firms and household decision making. Prior years some researchers had been carrying on observing experiments to the women and men labour work and in whose nature environment for weeks, and then used various treatments, including manipulating the environment in such a way to increase and decrease rest periods. They got result long time working hours and not rest time, it will reduce labours(workers) of productivity. So, it implies the overall productivity and individual productivity will be reduced. Although, the employers have enough workers to work in the natural working environment at the same time, but due to who have no enough rest time to provide to them, then their workers' working performance and efficiency will be fallen. Nowadays, industrialized countries had began to consider how to plan similar welfare reforms, researching the economic reasons and consequences to labour economic issue, such as United States, the United King, Sweden and Germany, it seems economic growth and law ethic has close relationship. However, labour economy includes how to measure labour's emotion to raise productivity, as well as how technological change, education, employment and wages which can assist labour to raise productivity. Due to good labour emotion and labour ethic can raise productivity, then raising productivity can also raise economic growth finally. So, I believe which have close cause and effect relationship.

However, many economists have long been pessimistic that an experimental approach could offer such illustrations of labour ethic and economic growth of cause and effect relationship in their field. Who feel labour bad emotion or bad labour ethic has no any influence to economic growth. In fact, the economic world is extremely complicated, so human needs to have economic laws is set by controlled experiment to measure or judge whether labour ethic and economic growth which has or has no any close relationship. If economists have no such test, economic laws, who can't perform such as the controlled experiments of chemists or biologists very well because who can't easily control other important factors to observe why labour emotion or ethic has reason to influence overall economic growth to any country if they neglect to carry on researching experiment between the relationship of ethic and productivity and economic growth. So I recommend economists need have participants in the natural field experiment to carry on researching to any labour emotion or ethic issue to gather statistic information of population to get prediction more accurately if who want to measure whether labour emotion or ethic and productivity which has close relationship to any country's economic growth for long term.

Why employers need to concern ethic to decide whether outsourcing is suitable to raise productivity growth to their businesses

Entrepreneurs need to concern whether outsourcing is suitable to whose entrepreneur culture. Generally, outsourcing can be defined as an organization is entering into a contract with another organization to operate and manage one or more of its business processes. Due to employers face increasing competitive pressure to remain focused, flexible, cost competitive and competent, so outsourcing can access to low cost specialized talent. However, outsourcing means the contracting out of a employer's non core, non efficient, non revenue producing activities to specialists.

It is a strategic management tool, such as restructure or contracting out to third party to carry out certain functions efficiently. The most common types of outsourcing are manufacturing outsourcing, information technology outsourcing and business process outsourcing (including processes related to accounting, human resources, benefits, payroll and finance etc. aspects). In fact, employers decide outsourcing reasons which include such as: market pressure to be price competitive, availability of cheap labour elsewhere, abundance of highly talented skilled labour in themselves country, pressure is from investing to cut cost, increase profit and show growth, focusing on core business operations and expanding global presence etc. factors. Many employers begin to concern the ethical and moral implication of outsourcing issue to cause the political and business discussion nowadays. Also, many economists have for-or-against social debates for outsourcing ethic issue. However, outsourcing can bring these benefits to some businesses. For example, if a car can be made more cheaper in China, it should be; if a telephone enquiry can be processed more cheaper in any Asia country, it should be. All such transactions raise real incomes on both sides as resources are advantageously redeployed, with added investment and growth in the exporting country, and lower prices in the importing country.

However, conservative economists argue that the sole mission of a corporation is to maximize profit for the benefits of shareholders. They also contend that in a global economy, outsourcing does not mean net job loss. They argue that more jobs will be created global since the cost labour lowered. The term "global" comes to mind when discussing today's large Corporations. It is hard to say which locally a company belongs to. In fact, outsourcing can also cause disadvantages. Sudden loss of jobs and loss of income can lead to economic depression in smaller regions. As the biggest employer in a those towns/cities closes down factories and start manufacturing in Asia or outsource the manufacturing altogether to a foreign this party. So, the country will raise unemployment rate suddenly when local jobs are outsourced to overseas.

Morality of local employees in favor of outsourcing hiring low wage employees elsewhere is another point of contention of this debate. The (capitalist) economy based on the law of supply and demand. In such economy, allocation or resources, including capital and labour is generally determined by market forces. Therefore, it is reasonable and expectable that companies would seek the best option available to employ their capital and recruit in a global economy. Due to it is assumed that local responsibility has less meaning when the economy and company operate globally. So, it causes any country employers don't concern labour ethic issue after outsourcing influences to its local labour.

Nowadays, many employers would agree that the acts of downsizing/ outsourcing for pure financial reasons (i.e. choosing short-term investor gain over employee welfare) are very often morally wrong. However, without clear morally relevant distinction (either in academia or business press) between a company's priority to the shareholder and that to its workers, it is very hard defend that position. This is justified because shareholders have taken a risk in placing their money in the hands of the corporation, and are thereby due compensation. Shareholders can potentially lose something who have placed into the corporation. However, workers have placed something at risk when accepting a job, they lose future potential earnings due to corporate outsourcing. At the very least, the worker has foregone other possible job opportunities. Even more importantly, many workers have invested in their houses, their local communities and in their lifestyle with the expectation of a steady income. When the worker's investment in a corporation is not of the same sort as the shareholder's, it constitutes a risk nevertheless, and so the worker's position is not different to that of the shareholder.

However, I believe that evaluating the differences of that risk will depend upon of each individual's relationship with the company and their personal values. For example, CEO pay is a completely separate issue on its own. It is a very popular subject in current academic and business press. Even if it is different subject, it has moral implications in regards to outsourcing. In general, CEO can earn a more percent raise to compare to regular worker's percent raise. In common, companies show the reason of CEO percent raise more is that there is enough causation to conclude that outsourcing contributes to profitability / stock price increase of a company, this the rise in CEO compensation. The ethic issue here is that, if the market rewards a company for improving it is bottom line or for cutting costs why is it ethically wrong for a company to outsource at the expense of local labour force. After all, the reason for an existence of company is to provide value to its shareholders. However, I think CEOs aims to achieve themselves benefits, who may improve their bottom line when hurting workers and communities. The morality of further rewarding CEO's who knowingly undertook layoffs of his employees in favor of outsourcing their work to a third party or move those jobs to a low wage country is very troubling.

In fact, outsourcing raises many concerns for working professional for and communities. It has long held personal and community values, such as , loyalty and commitment to employees. However, as much as economic prosperity global trade can bring, if does bring devastation as well. Availability of cheap products is appreciable, but you need to have a job and a income to consume those products. For many, outsourcing hurts at the heart of their livelihoods. Also, I argue to against outsourcing is that growing concern of issues of privacy related to outsourcing information creates an ethical and legal issue. The concern is against outsourcing (in specific cases of Accounting, Human Resource and Medical outsourcing) because of the fear of sensitive information's safety and confidentiality. So, employers ought check references and transcripts and perform background checks to minimize the risk of hiring someone who lacks ethic or morality to do whose outsourcing job duties. Moreover, outsourcing firms may indicate that all of their employees are highly educated, trained professionals of the highest honesty. Finally, I recommend employers ought to consider these questions before who decide to outsource, such as: does stockholders welfare out weight that of a company's employees? Is profit maximization ethical? Is it ethical to reward the upper management for cutting cost by eliminating jobs? Should the compensation for upper management with held if the profit is achieved by outsourcing? Is it ethical to reward a management that repeatedly shown disregard to its employees? (increasing workload, constant layoff, choosing the cheapest labour over quality). Is it right for the public to expect a company to keep all its employment locally, (at a higher cost) but at the same time sell products at comparable rate with foreign companies who use cheap labour? Does a company ethically bound a provide maximum occupation in its home country? Does it have a duty to its local community? In case of outsourcing is the employer ethically bound to retrain the employees? So, all these questions are very important concerning outsourcing influence, if every employer can concern these questions, then who can decide whose outsourcing reason is right or wrong more clearly. To conclude, any employer ought need to decide whether outsourcing is the best of one method to raise productivity for long term strategic plan.

How labour morality can reduce poverty in society to influence positive productivity to
whose performance

Entrepreneur needs to understand why labor morality concept can reduce poverty to influence positive productivity to raise performance. I shall use labour morality concept can assist society to reduce poverty to influence positive productivity to raise performance. In labour economy view, a livelihood comprises the capabilities of assets (including both material and social resources) and activities required for a means of living. A livelihood is sustainable when it can cope with and recover from shocks, maintain or enhance its capabilities and asset, when not undermining the natural resource base.

It has three elements: livelihood resources, livelihood strategies and institutional processes and organizational structures. So, I think that when productivity will raise, even poverty and crime will be also reduced, due to the low income level householder family which can be upgraded to increase whose income level and quality of living standard to the middle income level householder family. When governments can promote the labour morality to which employers to let them to know labour morality and productivity has close relationship.

How to understand the complex and differentiated process through which livelihoods are constructed, governments need to analyse which countries themselves local citizen to let their knowledge, perceptions and interests be heard. There are three insights into poverty as below:

The first is the realization that when economic growth may be essential for poverty reduction, there is not an automatic an automatic relationship between the two since if all depends on the capabilities of the poor to take advantage of expanding economic opportunities.

Secondly, there is the realization that poverty as conceived by the poor themselves. It is not just a question of low income, but also includes other factors, such as bad health, illiteracy, lack of social services etc.

Finally, it is now often know their situation and need best and must therefore be involved in the design of policies and project intended to better their lot. So, governments and employers need to identify those issues of subjects areas for effective poverty reduction, either at the local level or at the policy level. This is in principle on open-ended process, certain emphasis is given to the introduction of improved technologies as well as social and economic investments to every country's government.

The three fundamental attributes to any developing countries or developed countries themselves countries if which plan to raise economic growth and to reduce poverty to upgrade or low income level householders to rise to the middle income level householder family. The three attributes include the possession of human capabilities, such as education, skills, health, psychological orientation; access to tangible and intangible assets and the existence of economic activities.

However, a livelihood comprises the capabilities, assets, including both material and social resources and activities required for a means of living. A livelihood is sustainable when it can cope with and recover from stresses and shocks and maintain or enhance its capabilities and assets both now and in the future. To solve poverty problem, it includes not only physical and natural resources, but also every country's social and human capital issues. Every country's government also needs to facilitate an understanding of the causes of poverty by focusing on the variety of factors at different levels that directly or indirectly determine or constrain low income level householder's access to and assets of different kinds. Also every country's government needs to assess the direct and indirect effects on low income level householder's living conditions then, for example one dimensional productivity or income criteria.

Over the various components of a livelihood, the most complex is the portfolio of assets out of which people construct their living. This portfolio includes tangible assets, such as stores, e.g. food stocks, stores of value, such as gold, jewelry, cash saving and resources, e.g. land, water, trees, live stocks farm, equipment as well as intangible assets, such as claims, for example, demands and appeals which can be made be material, moral or other practical support and access, which is the opportunity to practice to use a resource, store or service or to obtain information, material, technology, employment, food or income.

Hence, if employers can provide enough capital input to make whose labours feel fairness, satisfactory and reasonable working environment and compensation. I believe that these satisfactory demand of labours who can raise productivity to their employers more easily. In labour economic view, any employers, governments or companies organizational resources inputs can divide four kinds of capital nature.

Firstly, the natural capital is natural resources stocks, e.g. soil, water, air, genetic resources etc. and environmental services, e.g. hydrological cycle, pollution sinks, etc. from which resources flows and services useful for livelihoods are derived . Secondly, economic or financial capital is the capital base, e.g. cash , credit/debt, savings and other economic assets, including basic infrastructure and production equipment and technologies which are essential for the pursuit of and livelihood strategy. Thirdly, human capital is the skill, knowledge, ability to labour and good health and physical capability important for the successful pursuit of different livelihood strategies and finally, social capital is the social resources, e.g. networks, social claims, social relations, which people draw when pursuit different livelihood strategies, requiring co-ordinated action. So, any country or employee which has a plan to know how to allocate which resources efficiently, it will raise productivity and economic growth and poverty reducing more easily. So, it seems labour morality can raise productivity which has close relationship to any employer, even labour morality and economic growth which has close relationship to any country. So, any country and any employer which ought not neglect labour morality for long term if who hope labor's producivity will raise and performance will raise efficiency.

TWO

THE HISTORICAL DEVELOPMENT OF BEHAVIORAL ECONOMICS TO ENTREPRENEUR'S ADVANTAGE

Entrepreneur needs to know whose employees' behavior and job attitude will be influenced by working environment. At the core of behavioral economics is used psychology of economics analysis to improve economics on its own terms generating theoretical insights, making better prediction of field phenomena, and suggesting better policy. It rejects economic theories based on utility maximization, equilibrium and efficiency. It is useful because it provides economists with a theoretical framework that can be applied to almost any form of economic (and even non-economic) behavior.

Simplifying much assumption that are not central to the economic theory. For example, there is nothing in core theory that specifies that people should not care about fairness, that they should weight risky outcomes in a linear fashion, or that they must discount the future at a constant rate. Other assumption simply acknowledge human limits on computational power and self-interest. These assumptions can be considered procedurally rational because human needs to solve problems that are often so complex that who can't be solved exactly by even modern computer technology.

Theories in behavioral economics should be judged by reality, generality and tractability concepts. We share the positivist view that the ultimate test of a theory is the accuracy of its predictions. But we also believe that better predictions are likely to result from theories with more realistic assumptions. In psychology, such as connectionist models that capture some of the essential features of neural functioning, which are based on utility maximization, yet are reaching the point where they are able to predict many judgement and behavioral phenomena. Contrary to the positivistic view, however, we believe that predictions of feelings (e.g., of subjective well-being) should be an important goal.

Most of the ideas in working behavioral economics environment are not new. When economics first became identified as a distinct field of study, psychology didn't exist as a discipline. For example, "invisible hand" and "the wealth of Nations" which belong to theory to moral sentiments, which laid out psychological principles of individual behavior that are arguably as profound as whose economic observations. Another example, such as a simple model of social utility means that one worker person's utility was affected by another person's payoff. However, the rejection of academic psychology by economists, which constructed an account of economic behavior built up from assumptions about the nature-that is, the psychology of homo-economics.

Nowadays, economists hoped their discipline could be like a natural science. But employee psychology was not very scientific. The economists thought it provided too unsteady a foundation for economics, who make assumption to utility led to a movement to the psychology from economics. In the early part of the 20th century, economists still included rich speculations about how employee behavior feel and think about economic choices generally. However, later economists are very much appealed to psychological insights, but by the middle of the century discussions of psychology had largely disappeared. Throughout the second half of the century, many criticisms of the positivistic perspective took place in both economics and psychology. The economists of the time had less disagreement with psychology with psychology than they realized. They assume without foundation that employee behavior always aims at the goal of maximum pleasure and minimum pain; but employee behavior is not goal-oriented. Also the economists of the time believed false conclusions are drawn from false psychological assumptions. The importance of psychological measures and bounds on rationality. These commentators attracted attention, but did not alter the fundamental direction of economics. One development was the rapid acceptance by economists of the expected utility and discounted utility models which are making decision under uncertainty and choice for organizations respectively. Whereas the assumptions and implications of utility analysis are rather flexible, and the expected utility and discounted utility models have numerous precise and testable implications. As a result, they provided some of the first "hand targets" for critics of the standard theory.

As economists began to accept counterexamples that could be not be permanently ignored, developments in psychology identified promising directions for new theory. Beginning around 1960 year, psychology became dominated by the brain as an information-processing device replacing the behaviorist conception of the brain as a stimulus-response machine. The information-processing permitted a fresh study of neglected topics like memory, problem solving and decision making. These new topics were more obviously relevant to the conception of utility maximization than behaviorism had appeared to be. However, employee psychologists began to use economic models as a benchmark against which their psychological models. Early research in employee behavioral have followed. First, identify assumption or models that are used by economists, who expected utility and discounted utility. Second, the assumption or model is a rule out alternative explanations (such as subjects' confusion or transactions costs). And third, the assumption or model creates alternative theories that generalize existing models. The fourth step is to construct economic models of behavior using the behavioral assumptions to test them from the third step. This final step of economic models of employee behavior has only been taken more recently to apply. Thus, it seems employee behaviors or performance will be influenced by organization environment.

Experimental control method measures consumption behavior

Entrepreneur needs to understand consumer individual consumption behavior will be influenced by organizational behvioral change environment. The methods in behavioral economics are the same as those in other areas of economies. In fact, behavioral economics relied heavily on evidence generated by experiments. More recently, however, behavioral economists have moved beyond experimentation and the full range of methods are employed by economists. The experiments played a large role in the initial phase of behavioral economics because experimental control is exceptionally helpful for distinguishing behavioral explanations from standard ones. I shall indicate the reasons why consumer consumption behavior will be influenced by organizational behavioral change environment as below:

Suppose we observed this phenomenon in these any one of cares, in the form of failures of legal cases to settle before trial, costly divorce proceedings, and labor strikes. They are phenomenon of human' behaviors are caused by costs and benefits measurement of result. Also, behavioral economy would be difficult to tell whether rejection of offers was the result of reputation-building in repeated games, agency problems (between clients and lawyers), confusion, or an expression of distaste for being treated unfairly. However, in these game experiments of failures of legal cases to settle before trial, costly divorce proceedings, and labor strikes.

The first three of these explanations are ruled out because the experiments are played once, have no agents, and are simple enough to rule out confusion. Thus, the experimental data clearly establish that subjects are expressing concern for fairness. Other experiments have been useful for testing whether judgment errors which individuals commonly make in psychology experiments also affect prices and quantities in markets. The lab is especially useful for these studies because individual and market-level data can be observed.

Although behavioral economists relied on experimental data, however, behavioral economics subject is seen as a very different method from experimental economics. As noted, behavioral economists are methodological profession. They define themselves, not on the basis of the research methods that who employ, but rather their application of psychological insights to economics. Experimental economists, on the other hand, define themselves on the basis of use of experimentation which is as a research tool. Also, economists have made a major investment in developing experimental methods that are suitable for addressing economic issues, and have achieving among themselves on a number of important issues. For example, experimental economists often make instructions and software available for precise replication, and raw data are typically shared for reanalysis.

Experimental economists also insist on paying performance-based. However, experimental economists have also developed rules that many behavioral economists are likely to find excessively . For example, experimental economists rarely collect data like demographics, self-reports, response times and other cognitive measure which behavioral economists have found useful. Descriptions of the experimental environment are usually abstract rather than which are carried on experiment in the outside world because economic theory rarely makes a prediction about how a happen would matter, and experimenters are concerned about losing control over incentives if choosing strategies with certain labels is appealing.

Finally, economic experiments also typically use "stationary replication", in which the same task is repeated over and over in each period. Data from the last few periods of the experiment are typically used to draw conclusions about equilibrium behavior outside the lab. When economists believe that examining consumption behavior after it is of great interest, it is also obvious that many important aspects of economic life are like the first few periods of an experiment rather than the last. Supposing if we need to make decision of marriage, educational decisions, and saving for retirement, or the purchase of large durables like houses, sailboats, can cars, which happen just a few times in a person's life, a focus on behavior is clearly not warranted. All said, the focus on psychological realism and economic applicability of research promoted by the behavioral-economics perspective suggests the usefulness research outside the lab and of a broader range of approaches to laboratory research. So, economists realize that who have ideal opportunity to learn by trial-and-error, in a stationary environment, and uses the opportunity to learn how to carry on experimenting any psychology and behavioral researches. Thus, consumption behavior will be influenced by external variable economy environment influences.

Judgement and choice influences behavioral consumption

Entrepreneur needs to understand consumer individual judgement and choice will influence behavioral consumption. The field of behavioral decision research, on which behavioral economics has drawn more than any other subfield of psychology, typically classifies research into two categories: judgement and choice. Judgement research deals with the processes people use to estimate probabilities. Choice deals with the processes people use to select among actions, considering of any relevant judgements who may have made. Everyday, we need to make probable judgements. Due to judging the likelihood of events is central to economic life. For example: Will you lose your job in a poor economic environment? Will you be able to find another house you like as much as the one you must bid for right away? Will the government raise interest rates? Will a merger strategy increase profits?

These questions are answered by some process of judging likelihood. The standard principles used in economic to model probability judgement in economic are concepts of statistical sampling, which are concerned probabilities in the face of new evidence. However, it requires a separation between previously judged probabilities and evaluations of new evidence. However, people often overestimate the probability who previously attached to events which later happened. This leads to "second guessing". For example, Monday morning quarterbacking and may be partly responsible for lawsuits against stockbrokers who lost money for their clients. (The clients think the brokers should have known). For example, anybody has tried to learn from a computer manual has seen the curse of knowledge in action. Another example for making probability judgements is called "representativeness": People judge conditional probabilities like P(hypothesis /data) or P(example/class) by how well the data represents the hypothesis or the example represents the class. Representativeness is an economical shortcut that delivers reasonable judgements with minimal effort in many cases. For example, in judging whether a certain student described in a profile is, say, a psychology major or computer science major, the student decides how well the profile matches the psychology or computer science .

For example, judgements of the fairness or non misleading or reasonable of clients' financial report to accounting auditors, consumers buying products and classroom negotiation. It is important to judge whether it is both a good attitude and bad attitude. A good attitude provides fast, close to optimal, answers when time or capabilities are limited, but it also needs logical principles and leads to situations. So, optimal is largely a critique (a reasonable one) of the later applied research. Assume that people specify a set of hypotheses, or encode new evidence incorrectly. For example, assuming that people believe hypothesis A is more likely than B will never encode pro-A evidence mistakenly, but will sometimes encode pro-B evidence as being supportive. For another example, investors will think there is wide variation in skill of, say, mutual-fund managers, even if there is no variation at all. (A manager who does well several years is a surprise if performance is mistakenly thought due to non replacement, so concluding that the manager must be really good.)

A question concerns stock market, such as: Overreacts in the long term. In their model, earnings follow a random walk but investors believe, mistakenly, that earnings have positive attitude. After one or two periods of good earnings, the stock market can not be confident that exists and hence expects, but since earnings are really a random walk, the stock market is too pessimistic and is underreacting to good earnings news. After a good earnings, however, the stock market believes many investors are increasing. Since, it is not the stock market is too optimistic and overreact. For another example, valuable consumer products (A $100 wireless keyboard, a fancy computer mouse, bottles of wine, and a box of chocolate) are sold to postgraduate (MBA) business students. The students were presented with a product and asked whether who would buy it for a price equal to the last two digits of their own social security number (a roughly random identification number required to obtain work in the United States) converted into a dollar figure, e.g. , if the last digits were 99, then the postgraduate business students will accept the hypothetical price was $99 to buy any of it for a price to the last two digits of their own social security number . After giving a yes/no response to the question. Would you pay $99? subjects were asked to state the most who would pay (using a procedure that gives people an incentive to say what who really would pay). Although subjects were reminded that the social security number is essentially random, those with high numbers were willing to pay more for the products. However, many studies have also shown that the method used to elicit preferences can have dramatic consequences. Nevertheless, when required to make an economic decisions-to-choose a brand of toothpaste, a car, a job, or how to invest, people do make some kind of decision. Behavioral economists refer to the process by which people make choices with ill defined preferences as "constructing preferences".

However, in classical consumer theory, preferences among different commodities are assumed to be invariant with respect to an individual's current consumption. Specifically, people seem to dislike losing commodities from their consumption much more than they like gaining other commodities. For example, the research of "contingent valuation" studies that attempt to establish the dollar value of products which are not routinely trades. Contingent valuation is often used to do government cost-benefit analysis or establish legal penalties from environment damage. These surveys typically show very large differences between buying prices (e.g. paying to clean up oil of beaches) and selling prices (e.g. having to be paid to allow beaches to be ruined). Thus, consumer judgement and choice will be influenced by external seller business behaviors and variable economy environment factors.

Nowadays, a quarter of the wealth in the USA has more interesting opportunities to do behavioral economies in consumption research. They find that motivated sellers should regard the price who paid as a sunk cost and choose at a nominal loss from the purchase price. Sellers' listing prices and subsequent selling behavior reflects to nominal losses. There are some cases in which no effect would be expected, such as when products are purchased for resale rather than for utilization. For example, do art or antique dealers like with pieces who buy to resell? What about surrogate mothers who agree to bear a child for a price paid in advance? However, evidence on the degree of commercial attachment is mixed. Reference points can also serve as social focal points for judging performance. For an interesting example from corporate finance. In general, when managers whose firms face possible losses (or declines from a previous year's earnings) are very reluctant to report small losses. As a result, the distribution of actual losses and gains show a very large at zero, and hardly any small reported losses (compared to the number of small gains). A manager who does not have the skill to shift accounting profits to erase a potential loss (i.e. has some earnings in his pocket.) is considered a poor manager. It seems that the bad performance manager whose behavior is bad to mislead public to believe his firm have better performance in this year.

Hence, in the mental accounting view, people set up mental accounts for outcomes which are psychologically separate, much as financial accountants lump expenses and revenues into separated accounts to guide managerial attention. Otherwise, mental accounting stands in opposition to the standard view in economics that it predicts, accurately , that people will spend money coming from different sources in different ways. So, a generalization of the notion of mental accounting is the concept of "choice bracket" , which refers to the fashion in which people make decisions narrowly, in either a piece meal fashion, or board, i.e. taking account of interdependencies between decisions. For example, when making many separate choices between products, consumers tend to choose more diversity when the choices are bracketed broadly than when they are bracketed narrowly.

Expected utility theory estimates behavioral consumption

Entrepreneur can apply expected utility theory to estimate consumer consumption behavior. The expected utility (EU) hypothesis explains that the utility of a risky distribution of outcomes (says, monetary payoffs) is a probability weighted average of the outcome utilities. It follows logically from apparently reasons. Most notably the independence (or " cancellation") choice. The independent choice says that if you are comparing two gambles, you should cancel events which lead to the same consequence with the same probability, your choice should be independent of those utility also simplifies matters because a person's taste for risky money distributions can be fully captured by the share of the utility function for money.

However, many studies document predictive failures of expected utility in simple situations in which subjects can earn substantial sums of money from their choices. Some of these new theories alter the way in which probabilities are weighted, but preserve a "between ness" property which says that if A is preferred to B, then any probabilistic gamble between them must be preferred to B, but dis preferred to A (i.e. the gambles like "between" A and B in preference). Other new theories suggest that probability weights are "rank-dependent", outcomes are first ranked, then their probabilities are weighted in a way which is sensitive to how who rank within the gamble that is being considered. For example, if a person is attitude towards gambles really came from the utility of wealth function, even large gains in wealth would not tempt who to risk $50 or $100 losses, if who really dislikes losing $10 more than who likes gaining $11 at every level of wealth. For example, linear probability weighting in expected utility (EU) works reasonably well except when outcome probabilities are very low or high. But low-probability events are important in the economy in the form of "gambles" with positive (lottery tickets and also risky business ventures in biotechnology and pharmaceuticals) and high risk compensation events which required large insurance industries. Another theory example, such as prospect theory is experimental choices more accurately than (EU) because it gets the psychological of judgement and choice right. It consists of two main components, a probability weighting function, and a "value function" which replaces the utility function of (EU). The weighting function P(P) combines two elements: (1) The level of probability weight is a way of expressing risk tastes (if you hate to gamble, you will place low weight on any chance of winning anything) and (2) P(P) captures how sensitive people are to differences in probabilities. If (a group consumers) people are move sensitive in the neigh hoods of possibility and certainty. i.e. changes in probability near zero and 1, then their P(P) curve will overweight low probabilities and underweight high ones. For another theory example, such as technical motivation for "rank dependent" theories, ranking outcomes, than weighting their probabilities is that when separate probabilities are weighted, it is easy to construct examples in which people will be dominance by choosing a "dominated" gamble A which has a lower chance of winning at each possible outcome amount, compared to the higher chance of winning the same outcome amount for a dominant gamble B.

If (consumers) people rarely choose such dominated gambles or the unique brands of products, who are acting as if who are weighting the differences in probabilities which is the essence of the rank dependent approaches. So, new information can help any decision maker to feel better to make better decisions. These theories effect may explain demand for information in settings like medicine or personal finance, where new information usually does not change choice, but relieves anxiety people have from knowing there is something who could know but don't. However, the planning problem for economic agents who would like to behave in fashion and discussed the important time discounting for choice. Most big decisions, e.g. savings, educational investments, labor supply, health and diet, crime and drug etc. decisions use have costs and benefits which occur at different point in time. Thus, time discounting is basically standard time discounting plus an immediacy effect, a decision discounts delays in equally at all moments except the current one, caring differently about well being. This functional form provides one sample and powerful model of the taste to individual to make right or reasonable behavior economic decision. However, most analyses of choice assume that people integrate new consumption with planned consumption. It is infeasible and perhaps for this reason, descriptively inaccurate. When people make decisions about new sequences of payments or consumption, they tend to evaluate them in isolation, e.g. treating negative outcomes as losses, rather than as reductions to their existing money flows or consumption plans.

How to decide fairness and social preferences. The assumption that people maximize their own wealth and other personal material goals just self-interest is a correct simplification that is often useful in economics. However, people may sometimes choose to spend their wealth to punish others who have harmed them, reward whose, so who have helped, or to make outcomes more fair. Just as understanding demand for products requires specific utility function, the key to understanding this sort of social preferences is a specification of social utility which can explain many types of date with a single function.

Behavioral economy can also use to assist firms to choose right behavior to decide to do any matters. I show hypothesis to establish any reference level of consumer surplus and product profit. Both sides are entitled to any firm's levels of profit, so price changes which threaten any matter are considered unfair. So raising any product price, it will reduce consumer surplus and is considered unfair. But the cost of a firm's inputs rises, subjects said it was fair to raise prices. Because not raising prices would reduce the firm's profit (compared to the reference profit). Everyday observation that firms don't change prices and wages as frequently commonly. For example, when the fourth Hary potter story book was released in summer 2000 year, most stores were allocated a small number of books that were pre-sold in advance. Why not raise prices or auction the books off? It is possible that it concerned about customer goodwill and excess demand to cause book stores limit such book price increases. Offended consumers are often able to affect firm behavior by media attention or provoking legislation. For example, scalping tickets for popular sports and entertainment events (resulting them at a large premium over the printed ticket price) is constrained by law in most countries. For example, some countries have "anti-laws" penalizing sellers who take advantage of shortages of water, fuel and other necessities by raising prices after natural disasters. So, the countries' governments can protect which citizen benefits to balance the natural resource supply and demand to sell in the reasonable price fairly after the natural disaster occurrence.

A few years ago, responding to public anger at rising CEO salaries when the economy was being restructured through downsizing and many workers lost their jobs. Otherwise, some countries passed a law prohibiting firms from deducting CEO salaries for tax purposes beyond $1 million a year. because the countries need to earn much tax income from these high salary CEO income every year. So, explaining why these laws and regulations come from is one example of now economics might be used to expand the scope of law and behavioral economic relationship.

How behavioral game theory influences shareholder's individual investment behavior

Entrepreneur needs to understand who can apply behavioral game theory to influence shareholder's individual investment behaviors. Game theory has rapidly become an important foundation for many areas of economic theory, such as bargaining in decentralized markets, contracting and organizational structure. The descriptive accuracy of game theory in these application can be questioned because equilibrium predictions often assume strategic reasoning and direct field tests are difficult. In fact, behavioral game theory uses any experimental evidence and psychological research to generalize the standard assumptions of game theory.

One component of behavioral game theory is a theory of social preferences for allocations of money to oneself and others. Another component is a theory of how people choose in one shot games or in the first period of a repeated game. For example, in share buying and selling market, shareholders shall buy or sell shares from their judgement in the economic cycle market everyday. So share investment is seemed as allocation of game to these shareholders. Also, shareholders whose mind can influence whose psychological behavior to decide how to invest whose shares in their share investment economic activities. The component of behavioral game theory can include a model of learning to either individual or a population. Also, game theory is one area of economy in which serious attention has been paid to the process by which can equilibrium comes about.

Many learning theories have been proposed and carefully tested with experimental data. Theories about population never predict as well as theories of individual learning through who are useful for other purposes. So, behavioral game theory can be applied to these complex environments. e.g. consumer supermarket purchase, share market etc. How to apply behavioral game theory to macroeconomics and saving aspect? Many concepts in macroeconomic probably have a behavioral style that could be influenced by research in psychology. For example, it is common to assume that prices and wages are in nominal terms, which has important implications for macroeconomic behavior. Behavioral economics suggests some ideas for among consumers and workers, perhaps it is influenced by workers' concern for fairness. An important model in macroeconomics is the life cycle model of savings or permanent income hypothesis. This theory assumes that people make a guess about their lifetime earnings profile, and plan their lifetime earnings profile, and plan their savings and consumption in each period has diminishing marginal utility; and preferences for consumptions streams are time-separable (i.e. overall utility is the sum of the discounted utility of consumption in each separate period). The theory also assumes people lump together different types income when they guess how much money who will have (i.e. different sources of wealth are different). So, why many young people won't spend too much money for unnecessary expenditure, e.g. entertainment easily. Because who plan to save for their old age to use in their long time life time.

In consumer personal consumption and shopping choice decision view point, a behavioral life cycle theory of savings in which different sources of income are kept track of in different mental accounts. Mental accounts can reflect natural perceptual or divisions. For example, it is possible to add up the travelers' pay check and dollar value of whose frequent flyer miles, but it is simply unnatural to do so. It is important to note that many key implications of the life-cycle hypothesis have never been well supported (e.g. consumption is far more closely related to current income than it should be according to theory. However, predictions can be improved by introducing utility functions with habit formation in which utility in a current depends on the reference point of previous consumption, and by more carefully accounting for uncertain about future income.

So, mental accounting is only one of several behavioral approaches that may prove useful. Economics is money illusion, it is the tendency to make decisions based on nominal quantities rather than converting those figures into real terms by adjusting for inflation. Money illusion seems to be pervasive in some domains. So, it appears that employees don't seem to mind if their real wage falls as long as their nominal wages doesn't fall. Labor macroeconomics is involuntary unemployment. Why can some people not find work beyond of switching jobs, or a natural rate of unemployment? A popular account of unemployment push that wages are deliberately paid above the market clearly level, which creates an excess supply of workers and hence unemployment. But why are wages too high ? As efficiency wage theory shows that paying workers more than who deserve is necessary to ensure that who have something to lose if they are unemployed, which motivates them to work hand and economizes on monitoring.

Another viewpoint indicates that employer and worker is such as into a gift exchange relationship. Employers pay more than who have to as a gift and workers repay the gift by working harder than necessary. They show how gift exchange can be an equilibrium and show some of its macroeconomic implications. In labor economics, gift exchange is clearly evident of experimental labor markets. In practical working environment, firms offer wages; workers who take the jobs than choose a level of effort, which is costly to the workers and valuable to the firms. For example, firms and workers can enforce wages, but not effort levels. Since workers and firms are matched for just one period, and do not learn each other's identities, there is no way for either side to build reputations or for firms to punish workers who chose low effort. However, self-interested workers should shirk, and firms should anticipate that and pay a low wage. In fact, firms deliberately pay high wages as gifts and workers choose higher effort levels when they take higher wage jobs. It seems that it has strong relationship between wages and effort is stable over time. For example, standard life-cycle theory assumes that if people can borrow they should prefer wage profiles which maximize the present value of lifetime wages. Holding total wage payments constant, and assuming a positive real rate of interest, present value maximization implies that workers should prefer declining wage profiles over increasing ones. However, in fact, most wages profiles are clearly rising over time which is such as a phenomenon. Rather, workers derive utility from positive changes in consumption, but have self-control problems. That would prevent them from positive changes in consumption, but have self-control problems that would prevent them from saving for later consumption of wages were more front-loaded in the life cycle. In addition, workers seem to derive positive utility from increasing wage profiles, it is perhaps because rising wages are a source of self-esteem and the desire for increasing payments is much weaker for non wage income.

The standard life-cycle of labor supply also implies that workers should substitute labor and leisure based on the wage rate who face and the value who place on leisure at different points in time. If wage fluctuations are temporary workers should work long hours when wages are high and short hours when wages are low. However, because changes in wages are often persisting and because work hours are generally fixed in the short-run. So, it is difficult to tell whether workers are substituting. For example, taxi drivers who target daily will drive longer hours on low income days and guilty early on high income days. This behavior is exactly the opposite of substitution. Also inexperienced taxi drivers support the daily targeting prediction. But experienced taxi drivers don't have negative elastic, either because target minded drivers earn less and self select or taxi drivers learn over time to substitute rather than target. Perhaps the simplest prediction of labor economics is that the supply of labor should be upward sloping in response to a increase in wage.

In finance, standard equilibrium models of asset pricing assume that investors only care about asset risks if who affect marginal publicly available information to forecast stock returns as accurately as possible the efficient markets hypothesis. When those hypotheses do make some accurate predictions and some investors in assets have limited rationality of behavioral finance. Also, in share stock market, it is common, shareholders should not want to trade with them, but the volume of stock market transaction is large. So, it presents data on individual trading behavior which suggests that the extremely high volume may be driven, in part, by overconfidence on the part of investors. For example, property agent's individual behavior is similar to share agent's individual behavior. In the economy view, property agent bases a list price for a house on the selling prices of nearly houses that is similar ("comparable"). Every nearest neigh our techniques bases on similarity is also used in credit scoring and other kinds of evaluations. Also, one firm whose every share sale on the selling price is comparable to its similar firms whose every share price in its same business industry. The shareholder will evaluate whose every share issued sale price in the stock (share) market. Otherwise, in behavioral economy view, for example, property or share buyer who has risky choice to decide to buy in the property or share market. It is a process of comparing the similarity of the probabilities and outcomes in two gambles and choosing on dimensions which are dissimilar.

As we mentioned above, behavioral economics simply includes an interest in psychology. In fact, we believe that many familiar economic distinctions do have a lot of behavioral content, they are implicitly behavioral, and could surely benefit from more explicit ties to psychological ideas and data. However, some people do not feel psychology and economy which have close relationship. Such as, substantial debate is ongoing in psychology about whether knowing the precise details of how the brain carries out computations is necessary to understand functions and mechanisms of driving car skill at higher levels, (knowing the mechanical details of how a car works may not be necessary to turn the key and drive it). Most psychology experiments use indirect measures like response times, error self reports and natural experiments, due to brain has been fairly successful in codifying what we know about thinking, but pessimists think brain scan studies won't add much. The optimists think the new tools will lead to some discoveries. Another couple is the distinction between short run and long run price elasticity which concerns behavioral economy. In fact, economy needs have theories concepts to support any evidence to prove any matter has happened. Concerning short run and long run price elasticity cause and effort issue, with a casual suggestion that the run is the time it takes for markets to adjust, or for consumers to learn new prices, after a demand or supply stock. Adjustment costs undoubtedly have technical and social component, but probably also have some behavioral factors influence in the form of gradual adaption to loss and learning.

Another macroeconomic model which can be interpreted as implicitly behavioral is that business cycles can emerge if it is not general price inflation, so why the consumers shall not decide to buy this kind of product in the competitive market. For example, risky choice is as a process of comparing the similarity of the probabilities and outcomes in two gambles, and choosing on dimensions which are dissimilar. Behavioral economic simply includes an interest in psychology. In fact, we believe that many familiar economic distinctions do have a lot of behavioral content, they are implicitly behavioral and could surely benefit from more explicit ties to psychological ideas and data. However, some people do not feel psychology and economy which have close relationship. Such as psychology is about whether knowing the precise details of how the brain carries out computations is necessary to understand functions and mechanisms at higher levels. (knowing the mechanical details of how a car works may not necessary to turn the key and drive it.) Most psychology experiments use indirect measures like response times, error rates, self reports and natural experiments due to brain has been fairly successful in codifying what we know about thinking. However, pessimists think brain scan studies won't add much. The optimists think the new tools will lead to some discoveries and the potential is great that they cannot be ignored. However, economy needs have theories or concepts to support evidence to prove why any matters had happened. An example, is the distinction between short term and long term price elasticity. This distinction, mentions between of them, with a casual suggestion that long run is the time it takes for markets to adjust, or for consumers to learn new prices, after a demand or supply shock. Adjustment costs undoubtedly have technical and social components, but probably also have some behavioral factors influence in the form of gradual adaption to loss and learning.

However, organizational behavioral theory concerns that organizational contracting are shot through with implicitly behavioral economics. Some economists motivate the incompleteness of contracts as a consequence of rationality in foreseeing the future, but do not tie the research directly to work on memory and imagination. For example, agency theory begins with the presumption that there is some activity the agent doesn't like to do. Why markets are better at making dramatic changes than managers influence cost. So, influence costs are the costs managers preform for projects who like or personally benefit from like promotion or raises. A lot of influence costs are undoubtedly inflated by optimistic, each division manager really does think their division desperately needs funds and social comparison of pay and benefits. Otherwise, why are salaries kept so secret? In all these cases, conventional economic behavior has deeper psychological questions of where adjustment costs, effort and influence costs come from. So, it beings these questions: Could these phenomena surely produce surprising testable prediction? Is psychology regularity an assumption or a conclusion?

Behavioral economics generally begins with assumption rooted in consumer psychological regularity and asks what follows from those assumptions. An alternative approach is to work backward, regarding a psychological regularity as a conclusion that must be proved an explanation that must be derived from deeper assumption before we fully understand and accept it. The alternative approach is caused by a fashionable new direction in economic theory and consumer psychology too, which is to explain human behavior as the product of evolution. However, we may not believe that behavior of intelligent, modern people lived in socialization and cultural influence can only be understood by guessing what their lives were like and how their brains might have adapted generally.

There are other models that treat psychological regularity as a conclusion to be proved rather than an assumption to be used. Such models usually begin with an observed regularity. Economists have for deriving behavior from first principles and rationalizing apparent irrationality. Theories of this sort are useful behavioral economics and what fresh predictions do they make. However, critics have pointed out that behavioral economics is not a unified theory, but is instead a collection of tools and ideas. This is true. However, some economists believe that economic models do not derive much predictive power from the single tool of utility maximization. The goal of behavioral economic is to develop better tools that, in some cases, can do both jobs at once. Economists like to point out the natural division of labor between scientific disciplines: Psychologists should concern to individual minds, and economists to behavior in games, markets, and economies. But the division of labor is only efficient if there is effective coordination, and all too often economists fail to conduct intellectual trade with those who have a comparative advantage in understanding individual human behavior. The only question is whether the implicit psychology in economics is good psychology or bad psychology. We think it is simply unwise, and inefficient to do economics without paying some attention to good psychology.

How to apply behavioral economic principles to make any business strategy

Entrepreneur needs to understand behavioral economy principles can be applied to himself/herself to judge to do the right decision more accurate. Behavioral economics theories can also apply to assist any policy makers to make right and reasonable decision in right time. I shall indicate new principles to recommend and I also shall give any psychological cases to explain how policy makers can apply behavioural economic theories to judge how to make their any decision is the most right and the most reasonable.

Behavioural economy is an independent and demonstrates real economic well-being. It aims to improve quality of life by promoting innovative solutions that challenge mainstream thinking on economic, environment and social issues. Also, behavioural economy is different branches of more alternative economies into a form that is useful primarily for policy-makers. I think behavioural economy can be given an aid to policy makers how who use economic tools to the broader policy making community by providing a theoretical behaviour for many policy approaches to be used. The standard economic analysis assumes that humans are rational and behave in a way to maximize their individual self-interest. This rational man assumption indicates a powerful tool for analysis. However, it has many shortfalls that can lead to unrealistic economic analysis and policy-making. Also, I think behavioural economics and psychology has these principles to influence human behaviour. These principles include, such as below:

In common, people do many things by observing others and copying; people are encouraged to continue to do things when they feel other people approve of their behaviour. People do many things without consciously thinking about time. These habits are hard to change. There are cases where money is de-motivating as it undermines people's intrinsic motivation. People want their actions and commitments to be values usually. People put undue weight on recent events and who can't calculate probabilities well and worry too much about unlikely events and who are strongly influences by how the problem/information is presented to them. People need to feel effective to make a change, even just giving who the incentives and information is not necessarily enough in any environment usually. So policy makers ought concern about these human behaviour principles to judge whose behaviours are right or wrong, then who can decide to do any economic activities more reasonable, e.g. decisions of consumption, policies making, investment etc.

In fact, much of our behaviour is strongly influenced by other people's behaviour. Social learning is a process by which we take in the behaviour of others to learn how to behave. In more complex situations with which we are unfamiliar, we consciously watch and learn from the behaviour of others. For example, when use a new library for the first time. When we make a conscious decision on how to behave, our sense of social identity is important, we think: how would other from my group behave in this situation? In situations where there is high social capital. i.e. where there are strong networks between people and a high level of mutual trust, so its seems other people's behaviour and our sense of social identity may be extremely important in influencing our own behaviour and policy makers ought need to know how to judge their behaviour whether their behaviour is either right and reasonable or wrong and unreasonable in any learning process of environment. The standard economic theory is tried to explain where people's preferences come from, so it does not take account of the direct influence of the people's behaviour and social norms on our behaviour. The theory assumes we independently know what we want and that our preferences are fixed. This standard theory is very good at explaining short-term decision making. For example, I want green vegetables and choose fruits as they are on special offer, but it cannot explain longer term changes in preferences. I now only choose organic food. Along the same lines the importance of institutions, such as regulations, for example, how people organize markets and the evolution of the whole economic system are not subjects of general economic analysis. This has significant implications for policy design.

In fact, the standard economic theory also assumes that people carry out a full rational analysis of all consumers' available options. This is not what we do; we often just copy the actions of other people. For example, it would require too much effort to look up all the rules when driving in a new country, to find out all the fines/punishments for failing to meet the rules, to work out the probability of being caught and the possible costs, before deciding how to drive there. Instead we just copy other people, and perhaps adjust our behaviour according to the feedback we receive. However, some psychologists indicate to see people how to behave, in especial in crises situations and when others are experts. These psychologists have identified that we are open to influence from people in authority or people we like. When we are influenced by authority, an expert, someone with legitimate power to direct our actions, someone who can either reward or punish us. The effects are less likely to be lasting than we are influenced by someone we like.

However, some people's psychological behaviour is similar to economic behaviour to judge to make any decision. For example, why do you wear a seatbelt in your car? Most of us wear seatbelts as it has became normal behaviour, everyone does it. We neither evaluate the likelihood of having an accident, nor the chance of getting caught without our seatbelt on and incurring a fine. The enforcement of seatbelt wearing is now hardly necessary, as it has become a social norm. What does this mean for policy makers? Policy makers focusing only on economic analysis may often devise a system that has an immediate effect. In psychologists view this issue point, knowing that there is a fine for speeding and a high likelihood of getting caught, the driver will probably drive more slowly, but who will drive just as fast one who realize the chance of being caught is low. However, of policy makers can change the social norm, perhaps in this case by encouraging us to frown on others who drive dangerously fast with campaigns against dangerous driving, then less enforcement will be needed after the change. In other words policy makers might want to take preferences as fixed in the short term, but they should consider shifting preferences in the medium term. An example where policy appears to have successfully changes people's preferences in the US and Singapore and Hong Kong is banning smoking in public places. This change appears to reduce the social proof of the amount people smoke in private places and public places both also.

It seems that government policies can influence the decreasing numbers of consumers require to buy cigarette to smoke habitually, due to fine and punishment is regulated to be ban effectively. Such daily routines quickly became habits. Even when we consciously think about what we do, it can be difficult to change our behaviour. Perhaps I think it is a good idea for people to use public transport, but I do not know where the bus stop is or when the bus runs. I think to use private car to drive to work place is more preference choice. The reward feeling , my journey by car was easy and free to reinforce my old bad habit. Psychologists theories on changing habits generally involve raising it to a conscious level where we can consider the merits of alternative behaviour. This is followed by adopting the new behaviour, which, with time, becomes frozen as a new habit. Thus, I think that we need have regulation to control my behaviour, then we can change my behaviour to be new habit from old habit of behaviour easily. For example, human blood sale is an economic product, due to paying donors for blood would increase supply. Supplies would be provided at a cost advantage in the future, if demand continued to rise. Such as supplies to hospitals for blood will has cost from donors when there are many patients need much blood to use to treat any diseases in any hospitals. Otherwise, if there are not many patients need much blood to use, but there are many donors have effort to provide blood to any hospitals, then it will be economic inefficiency and it is highly wasteful of blood. Thus, the blood donors whose blood supplies of behaviour and the cost of blood which will concern to the hospitals patients' numbers of demand, so their behaviour and economy has close relationship in the hospital blood demand market.

For shareholder behaviour example, if you hold some shares in a firm that has gone down in value. What do you do? Many people hold on to their shares in this situation, in the hope that they will recoup their losses. Conversely, when shares have gone up in share, people are happy to sell them to realize their gain, A similar behaviour is also observed for professional traders who tend to hold on to shares with a loss for longer than those with a gain. The traders who exhibit this type of loss to a lesser degree tend to be the more successful ones. For another example, this is a case where the theory is directly applicable within economic cost-benefit-type analyses that include valuations of no-market products, such as valuations of pollution damage. Policy makers have a choice as to whether-to-accept, and as these may vary by up to a factor, the outcome of such an analysis many well depend on which value is chosen. When a policy maker reasonably has a right to something that might be taken away from them, the willing-to-accept value would be used. On the other hand, when the policy maker only reasonable has a right to the status quo and an improvement is proposed, then the willingness-to-pay is the correct value to use.

What behavioral economic preferences regarding time discounting theory would pay and the conclude that the discounted psychologists have long established utility model, which continues to be that people don't make decisions in widely used by economists, has little the way assumed. In generally, people are expected to rationally make the best choices given their preferences, independent of how these choices are presented. Therefor more information and choice is always considered good. Using this theory, policy makers should ensure that people always have as much information and as many things to choose between as possible, the process of introducing policy is irrelevant. Ideas from behavioral economic indicate, however that this is not the right approach.

However, we know from experimental economics that more choice and more information can lead to a feeling of helplessness or reduced self-efficiency. Hence, if people hope have better solutions to a problem. Instead, providing people with opportunities for understanding, exploration and participation engages powerful motivations for competence, being needed. In summary, people 's self-efficacy increases and they are motivated toward implementing the solutions. i.e. changing their behaviour in a desired way. So, a participatory approach not only improves policy, it also makes to any policy makers more happier. In most cases these principles cannot be used directly as part of any mathematical economics analysis, but highlight situations where this standard analysis will not accurately describe human behaviour and therefore might have unintended consequences when implemented in policy. However, that the policy implications could be quite powerful as the behavioural approach provides quite different lines of analysis to the standard economic model. It is heartening to see policy makers focusing more on the psychology of behaviour when devising policy. So behavioural economics is a relatively new field of economics that attempts to incorporate insights from psychology into economic models and analyses. As above cases seem any policy maker's economic activities which are relative to whose psychology's decision. However, psychologists are often interest in understanding at the level of individual or social group of behaviour, the primary interest in economic is usually in understanding how behaviour and interactions play out in a system to shape economic outcomes. Economists are interested in system-level outcomes, such as the level and path of wages, the effect of taxes on economic output, how rates of savings respond to interest rates etc. However, those economic outcomes depend on complex interactions of individuals. So, behavioural economy concerns to how to judge individual to do the reasonable or right behaviour to hope to get the reasonable economic result as well as it's goal rather to help improve any policy makers to understand their behaviour in ways that allow economists to make better predictions and suggest better economic policies. However, new elements about information processing or individual preferences might impact economic models and analyses.

Is psychology influencing all field of economics? It is possible that behavioural economy needs theoretical contributions and laboratory evidence to support to make any reasonable or right decision to any policy makers. This type of work generally uses existing observational data and estimates relationships between variables of interest by either using naturally occurring variation in the data i.e. natural experiment. Perhaps more than any other field, behavioural economics has had a large impact on finance to the point that behaviour finance is often considered a separate field as opposed to being of behavioural economics. Also, public economic is the study of how government policies influence economic markets. A primary emphasis of public economic involves the topic of taxation. Otherwise, the biggest impact that the behavioural approach has had in economic is the analysis of retirement saving to influence any employees' decisions about their retirement savings. However, when employees can do make any active savings choices to prepare their retirement. If employers can assist whose employees to design any methods to allocate fund, then accumulates interest and is tax free until the retirement funds are withdrawn to every retirement employee. The tax advantage make effort to save for retirement.

Behavioural economic is in understanding how individuals do or do not smooth consumption over time. Smoothing consumption is a standard economic models. It suggests that individuals should borrow or save in order to consume a similar amount throughout one's lifetime. For example, a teacher who is paid a salary 12 months a year, who should not spend all whose salary within one year. Rather, the teacher should smooth whose consumption over the 12 month period. How to allocate to spend pay checks, food and social security payments which concerns the teacher decide to spend whose salary efficiently. Hence, who needs to plan how he shall spend whose one year salary to be reasonable use in the future. Public economic is to understand how people respond to taxation and social benefit programs. This has been an area that has seen an explosion of behavioural work in recent year. i.e. how taxpayers can experience over-withholding and receive tax refunds from tax department.

Policymakers and insurers are also increasingly turning to psychology for approaches to improve health behaviour. Traditionally health-policy focused largely on information provision, assuming that as long as individuals were well informed, their decisions would maximize their health choices. Influential work on the effects of smoking taxes, however, well being of smokers appears to increase with higher taxes to influence health behaviours are not completely rational.

Behavioural economic has also had a small impact on the study of criminal behaviour. For example, individuals are not less likely to commit a crime when who are 18 age and of doing so increases dramatically. However, some economists explain the motivations people have for giving to charity and who understand the psychological motivations for charitable giving. So, it seems that charity award giving has probable to reduce 18 age people who choose to do crime behaviour easily because who feel who have effort to assist charity in their life time.

Industrial organization economists study why firms exist and how which function and compete with each other. Insights and psychology and behavioural economics have made a significant contribution to develop that model the interactions of profit maximizing firms with their customers. In fact, firms often need to evaluate whether their products if prices are needed to set what of price of level is the most reasonable and attractive to customers to choose to buy their products. For example, individuals choose cell phone plans with fixed minute allotments and steep charges for going over the minute limits, but frequently exceed their plan limits. This behaviour is the best explained by a model in which people overestimate the precision of their demand forecasts. So, cell phone firms need to research how cell phone plans with fixed minute allotments and steep charges of cell phone call fee charge plan is the most acceptance method to cell phone clients generally. However, cell phone call charge plan and various cell phone product features and the way cell phone clients allocate their limited attention affects cell phone products markets which are external important factors can influence any cell phone clients why who will choose to use the cell phone call plan because any cell phone will be very large durable product to any cell phone consumer after who choose to buy the cell phone product. Hence, who will not often choose to use the old cell phone firm call charge plan if who feel it provides the excellent cell phone call service and reasonable phone call plan to use to compare other cell phone call plans in the cell phone call market. Hence, the cell phone call firm needs to research why consumers need to choose to use which cell phone call plan among of other cell phone call plans in the cell phone call market. Also, researching the cell phone buyers' choice behaviour why who choose to buy the cell phone to use issue, which will have influence to the cell phone buyer why who choose to use the cell phone call charge plan because expensive cell phone is needed to use excellent quality of cell phone call service usually. Otherwise, cheap cell phone is needed to use poor quality of cell phone call service usually. So, cell phone call plan is needed to follow the cell phone quality and price to be used and they ought have direct relationship to influence why the cell phone buyer who chooses to use the cell phone call plan.

Finally, behavioural economic can also apply to be used to labour supply as a motivating in negative or positive labour supply elasticities example. For example, it is possible that taxi drivers work fewer hours when wages are high-consistent with a model of daily income targeting. This finding is that when wages are high (perhaps it is raining and thus it is easy to find people who want a taxi ride), taxi drivers are able to hit their daily target quickly and then go home. However, when wages are low, taxi drivers are not able to hit their target quickly and thus work additional hours in order to hit their target. It means taxi driver's behaviour produce the effect that taxi driver works more when wages are low than when wagers are high. This work has resulted to analyse taxi driver of labour supply decisions with daily reference points in non taxi domains. So, instead of the weather and client numbers and taxi charge factors, the factors of taxi drivers' hours worked and the quality of service is produced is another important factor to influence any taxi drivers' numbers to supply to the taxi market.

Behavioural economic has also influenced the understanding of how staffs can impact worker productivity and job satisfaction. For example, it is possible that poor cooperation can cause worker productivity decreases and it can also cause poor job satisfaction to the worker. So, when working environment can impact productivity, social comparisons can have an impact on job satisfaction as well as the worker's job satisfaction and search intentions are affected by knowing about the salaries of their peers in whose firm. Hence, the worker's positive or negative psychological feeling to whose employers which will have effort to influence whose working performance and productivity to whose firm in possible.

Behavioural economic is increasingly being used in the field of development economics or low income countries. Such as, how Philippines can offer commitment to individuals who wanted to save money in whose country or how Philippines can change to smoking behaviour when commitment devices were offered to Philippine smokers. So, Philippines policy makers need to concern resource scarcity and resource allocation issue to solve how to let its low income level householders can raise to the middle income level to achieve the high income level householders and the low income level householders whose income level is not distant very much.

Behavioural economy and business strategy relationship

Why behavioural economy and business strategy which has cause and effect relationship. This is any entrepreneur's psychological issue. I shall analyze whether the relationship between the discipline of behavioural economy and psychology which two branches are totally opposite or if the behavioural theories only extend and complement that mainstream economics. I think study of economics is the behaviour of the complex human beings; this science examines how people choose to act and allocate resources in different market situations. So the economic analysis, is based on the implications that arise from a series of simple assumptions (which are sometimes cited as unrealistic) regarding the human nature. However, in psychological view, the individual is characterized by unlimited rationality and by the ability to follow time consistent, in every situation, his self-interest.

In these conditions, behavioural economic attempts to consider a field of analysis in the study of economic phenomena. Because economics deals with the study of human behaviour on the market, it highlights the human character of the science and the fact that, besides of all the patterns and models, the analysis refers to the real individual. It is also behavioural because it attempts to combine approaches from several sciences mainly from economics and psychology, and also from sociology, philosophy, anthropology or biology. This is not an easy mission, in the conditions in which these various disciplines have adopted in time different approaches that became, in many ways, contradictory. So, behavioural economics is that a multidisciplinary approach will increase the explanatory power of economics.

On one hand, there are specialists two argue that behavioural economic is a field of economics that continues the hand, there are others who see it as a distinctive school of thought, which proposes a new paradigm. However, behavioural economists propose a multidisciplinary study, criticize certain assumptions on which the traditional model is built (such as rationality and self-interest, in their unlimited form), resource to experiments (the classical method of psychology) to validate some assumptions, propose new theories (such as the prospect theory) and advance different interpretations of the economic behaviour, e.g. how to maximize consumers satisfy their needs. This issue is concerned to concern consumption of psychology and social economic situation research aspect. Also, I think that behavioural economics can help the economic science by describing more realistically the utility functions of the individuals.

This field of study is based rather it is a natural extension of the basic approach. However, it is can be claimed that behavioural economics is also built on the premise that psychology methods and assumptions are equally important. Also, models of behavioural economics, allow the utility to depend on the differences between one's own level and a reference level. People are sensitive to changes and preferences are not stable in time. The vision of behavioural economics concerning the inter-temporal choice (which assumes that individuals prefer immediate gains and delay unpleasant activities) seems to be more appropriate to the human behaviour that the one of the traditional model (which assumes that utility is updated over time).

In conclusion, I shall indicate two theories to explain why economy and psychology has close relationship to influence human do any behavioural economic activities daily. For example, through the prospect theory, behavioural economics adds new parameters to improve the mathematical modelling method, which was advanced by economists for decisions taken under uncertainty. However, the theory also proposes a slightly different interpretation. The results are interpreted by the individual as positive or negative deviations from a reference point, which has a neutral psychological value. Last but not least, in addressing social preferences, behavioural economics adds parameters that increase the concern of decision-makers to also assess their utility function in relation to others.

For another example, the choice theory; secondly there is not a common consensus between the specialists of behavioural economics regarding the variables that should be included; and finally, many variables that affect the behaviour are not quantitative, but qualitative, and cannot be precisely measured. The findings of behavioural economic are relevant and can help the mainstream theory by providing a more realistically base of study.

However, this argument has contributed to the development of behavioural economics, because there are a large number of phenomena that cannot be entirely explained by the mainstream economics. So, why in the beginning, I indicated why behavioural economics does not imply the totally exclusion of the neoclassical approach and the most studies in this area try to provide a more realistic base of the standard theory. In the concluding, I believe that in time, behavioural economic models will replace the simplified ones, based on unlimited rationality. Also, economists have provided a great importance to the quantitative structures, departing from the human nature. However, behavioural economics can become truly revolutionary only it will always be receptive and will provide a critical insight to their own theories and perspectives, and especially the ones regarding the aspects that they reproach to the traditional economic theory. However, I also feel that the individual's behaviour on the market is determined only be economic factors. In brief, individual choices and, by this, the demand variation are explained only and the variations in the prices of products/services and the available personal income. Am important discussion in the field of determine directly the economic behaviour of an individual (like the sociological and psychological of factors) are actually active elements in the process the reshaping of the utility functions. Finally, in my view, I believe that the conduct of the market phenomena, as it occurs in reality. In this sense, the research of behavioural economics aims to see how the neoclassical model could be improved, using mainly psychology concepts. Although, there are some specialists who argue that behavioural economics can be an alternative to the neoclassical theory.

Most findings of my study conducted in this research, modify some of standard economical assumptions, in order to provide a greater psychological realism. However, the additions proposed by behavioural economists simply recognize the human limitations on (mentally) calculations, will and self-interest. So, I think psychology and economy has close relationship to influence any policy makers or decision makers to do any economic psychology daily. Because the purpose of economics is to better understand and explain the conduct of the economic activities as which occur in reality. Otherwise, human being is complex and its behaviour and constitution is studied by all the social sciences. Consequently, multi and interdisciplinary approaches can bring real benefits to the economic science, by providing a more realist foundation to cause any policy makers or decision makers how to decide to make any behaviours or economic activities by behavioural economic activities support daily.

THREE

HOW LABOR BEHAVIOR INFLUENCES EFFICIENCY

Why labour behavior can influence efficieny?Economics of risky health behaviours can include these personal behaviour, such as smoking, drinking alcohol, drug use, unprotected sex and poor diets is a major source of preventable death. How traditional economics approaches emphasize utility maximization, under certain assumptions which is result of a limited role for policy interventions. Also, non traditional models, e.g. hyperbolic time discounting or bonded rationality how government intervention has greater potential to increase social welfare.

The consequences of risky health behaviours for economic outcomes, such as medical care cost, educational cost, employment wages and crime. Also how policies and strategies modify risky health behaviours, such as taxes or subsidies, cash incentives, restrictions on purchase and use, providing information and restricting advertisement etc. government intervention behaviour. Why health behaviours are important. Because health market includes market products and services, such as medical care, investments of time, environmental conditions, such as air pollution, sanitation and water purity. In special, industrial countries need to concern morality more than infections diseases, health behaviours are particularly important. However, alcohol consumption is also serious in developed countries, e.g. United States, England.

Why is health behaviour important? Because tobacco smoking, diet, physical activity and alcohol and drug consumption and useful sexual behaviours, driving and illicit drug use etc. unhealthy behaviour or consumption is increasing to cause many people to be dead easily in developing countries and developed countries both. As a result, many of the risk factors may reflect a combination of health behaviours and medical treatments. For example, high blood pressure has risk factor to be affected by health behaviour, such as smoking, physical in activity and diet. In fact, the risks of death included child underweight, unsafe water sanitation and indoor smoke for solid fuels which are a direct consequence of poverty. However, poverty could affect unhealthy behaviours. So, low income household families play roles of high risk factors to cause who choose to do unhealthy behavior to cause death easily.

Health behaviours, such as physical in activity (no leisure-time physical activity), medical screening tests. Overall, changes in health behaviours since the 1970 year, particularly the rapid decline in smoking have mostly operated in the direction of improving overall health. However, the race/ ethnicity, age, education and annual family income factors can influence health behaviours. Usually, high income and education and Western or Asia race people who are more concerning about their health. So, the countries' governments can spend less expenditure on medical welfare assistance to prepare to them to use when who are old age to reach retirement time. Although, these countries' governments can expand less medical expenditure to give welfare to these kind of people, but their hospitals income will be also decreasing, due to these high income and educational people who are concerning their health to avoid to eat bad foods and eat the health foods, so their sick will be also increasing in their life time, it means that who will not often see doctors, so hospitals' income will also decrease because which will decrease these patient numbers often.

However, differences in health behaviours are one possible explanation for why socio-economic status is positively related to health status and life expectancy. So, it can explain that behaviour is only a small fraction of the better health and longer life expectancy experienced by high individuals with high socio-economic status. It seems behavioural choices increase the estimated effect of behaviours on health outcomes and reduce the death or illness causes. For example, high educated people began to concern to eat health foods, e.g. fruits and vegetables between 1988 year to 1994 year and 1999 year to 2002 year. Hence, it can cause the fresh foods, e.g. vegetables and fruits markets consumption increased, due to the high educational consumers of numbers are increasing because who began to change diet behaviours to choose to buy much fruits or vegetables to eat daily. It is possible that who began to believe those are health foods. Also, some liking driving consumers who liked to drive cars to be relax in their entertainment time. However, due to many doctors promote health message from televisions or radios or newspapers or sport magazines etc. media, such as often walking, running, riding bicycles sports are more health to any people to cause long time life easily. So, these often driving consumers will reduce much time to drive their cars in their leisure or rest time on Sunday or Saturday or holidays. However, who will choose to carry on walking or running or riding bicycles in their leisure or rest time often. So, their physical activities are changed to do sport behaviour from driving their cars of behaviour because who feel sport can be health to them. Otherwise, driving is not health to them. It will cause the oil, gas, electric battery car energy supplied companies income will be decreased because who will not spend much expenditure to buy these energy power to drive their cars often. So, these driving householder families consumer numbers will be decreasing when who choose to spend their rest or relax time to change their driving behaviour to do health physical activities often. It seems consumers who change their behaviours can influence the product or service suppliers' income in possible. So, it seems that consumer health behaviours can caused some businessmen income will be increased, such as vegetables or fruits foods. Otherwise, the beefs foods businessman income will be decreased. When the many consumers change their diet behaviours immediately. For another example, the smoke companies income will be decreased, when many smokers choose to reduce their smoking of numbers every day. Also, the hospitals income will be decreased if many people are health and who have no any diseases, e.g. cancer. So, hospital cancer patients of numbers will reduce. Also, it is possible that hospitals will not employ many cancer doctors because cancer patients of numbers decrease immediately. But in the long term, these countries' governments will avoid to spend much medical welfare allowance to assist many poor householder or low income householder families in the future because it is possible that these are many cancer patients of numbers will decrease. Also, the countries' air pollution will be reduced due to less people have smoke habit. For another example, when many liking driving people who reduce time to drive cars in their relax or rest time when who do not need to drive to work. So, their cars won't need much oil or gas or electric battery power to consume, it means that these power suppliers will decrease to sell private car oil or gas or electronic battery products to these liking driving householder families. So, it seems consumers' health behaviour can influence the economic income to some businessmen.

The importance of health behaviour in explaining morality in economically developed countries. Smoking, alcohol consumption, drug use consumption behaviours are economic concepts that relate to all behaviours and the important differences across the various health behaviours. The traditional economic approach to studying health behaviours. Basic aspects of the model are that people receive health capital at birth, which depreciates with age, but can be raised through investment, death occurs when the health stock falls below a minimum level. Health has both consumption and investment aspects, as life time is available for market and non market activities. People produce health by combining market products and services with time. For example, on individual might choose to buy sport running shoes and spending time to run on their rest time for relax on Sunday, Saturday or holiday. Individual can allocate time and money to maximize the present discounted value of lifetime utility. Indirectly, length of life is a choice in the original model.

Specially, the timing of death results from conscious decisions regarding health investments made with full knowledge of health education. Assuming that health has only investment aspects, i.e. it doesn't enter the utility function directly and is only valuable for producing healthy days. Health capital is characterized by an equality of the supply of health capital, i.e. the opportunity cost of health capital and the demand for health capital, i.e. the marginal monetary return on health investment. Usually, people invest in such behaviours until the margin, the return on investments in health equals the opportunity cost of health capital.

The model also applies to unhealthy behaviours, as negative investments in health. The marginal costs of the unhealthy behaviour, including both the monetary cost of purchasing market products, such as cigarettes and alcohol and cost of reduced health and shorter life time and the marginal benefits, such as the pleasure derived from consumption of these unhealthy market products, such etc. However, schooling may improve health by enhancing allocative efficiency (participation in healthier behaviours) or productive efficiency (obtaining more health from the same set of inputs). Economists have used a variety of identification strategies to measure the causal effect of education on health behaviours. In the past, schooling concentrated on measure the causal unhealthy behaviours on smoking, but it neglected to measure the causal unhealthy behaviours on drinking alcohol, unhealthy diet and drug mislead. The habit and addition can cause unhealthy behaviour to anyone daily.

The marginal utility of current consumption rises with the stock of past consumption to cause habit consumption. So, why the smokers who can not choose to buy any cigarettes to smoke or alcohol to drink easily because whose past buying behaviours are caused to habitual consumption. For example, the first time, an individual consumes the addictive substance, who has a stock of past consumption of zero, but after the individual has been heavy user for sufficiently long to have the maximum stock of past consumption when whose consumption is not only for below the utility who enjoyed during whose first use of additive substance. Hence, this past consumption behaviour has become habitual over longer periods of time.

However, concerning responsiveness of consumption to price, consumption at a point in time is related not only to current prices, but also to past prices. So if permanent price changes can affect demand more than temporary ones because forward-looking persons anticipate and make decisions based on future dynamics in prices. Moreover, the price elasticity of demand for the additive product will be greater in the long run than in the short run and that difference will rise with the level of addictiveness. Specifically, if a rise in price of unhealthy products, such as cigarettes and alcohol that which is expected to cause less consumption in the future. So it becomes optimal to hold a lower quantity of addictive stock, which is achieved by reducing consumption to habitual behaviours.

Rational choice theory assumes that consumers make choices, such that their utility is maximised, subjects to budget constraints. Under rational choice theory, regulation which relaxes budget constraints, increases income, alters relative prices or changes consumer preferences will be effective in changing behaviour. Hence, behavioural economics draws on psychology and behavioural sciences in assessing consumer behaviour. So, social and emotional variables can impact on choice. For example, including simple message which reinforce social norms was found to influence electricity consumption. Such as bad health to smoking or often sit down driving private cars on rest time habits is also good message to reduce consumers who spend too much time to carry on bad health behaving. Under these conditions, some evidence suggests that interventions can be:

cost-effective relative to more direct or traditional government intervention, used existing regulatory approaches, targeted in influence and easy to implement. When behavioural economics and rational choice theory provide a useful foundation for policy makers, however both theories also face challenges in their application to regulatory design. So, policy makers ought consider to the specific of markets and market participants when applying any form of consumer theory for purposes of designing and predicting the effects of regulatory policy.

Rational choice theory means consumers rank preferences over all products, makes consumption choices based on these ranking, such their utility is maximized. It is further assumed that individuals rationally pursue their self-interest subject to all economics constraints, such as time, income and capital. Rational choice theory is both positive or negative attitude to any consumer. it seeks to describe how people do behaviour and also how who ought to behave. It will impact on consumer behaviour when it relaxes the consumer's budget constraint, alters prices of products and/or services, e.g. mobile gas price or private car price, smoking price and/or influences a consumer's preferences, such as through information disclosure. Examples of those type of regulation include: financial (dis)incentives, banning or limiting choices, and/or requiring the disclosure of certain information. So, behavioural economics is essentially a series of observations about how people do behaviour in certain situations. It is therefore purely positive. For example, why consumers like to choose to smoke, although who know smoking has bad influence to whose health or why consumers like often drive private cars on rest or relax time on Sunday or Saturday or holiday, although who know who need to pay much gas, even who will lose time to do sport and it is tired to them to drive their private cars often.

Rational choice theory indicates any consumer needs to understand all prices, including opportunity costs, preferences and constraints to make comparison to decide whether who will choose to buy the product or enjoy the service. Could behavioural economics help improve diet quality for nutrition to raise any consumer health? Recognizing that consumption choices are determined by factors other than prices, income and information for consumers' food choices. How to make food choices that promote health and prevent disease. Food manufacturers and marketers have discovered that certain psychological cues, such as packaging and presentation are efficient ways to increase consumption of their products. Could similar marketing approaches be used in public health efforts to improve diet quality and reduce body weight. So, improving diet quality among any nutrition program has the potential to guide food choices at a critical time, when a child's dietary preferences are being defined. For example, letting students preselect menu options to school lunch or school breakfast programs or giving food stamp participants the options to pre order groceries by telephone or online may improve the healthfulness of their food students with parents or guardians could specify purchased with prepaid cards. So, students will consume to select using prepayment (fixed costs), those school nutrition dietary preference often then choice that can be purchased only with cash (variable costs). Hence, this consumption behaviour will influence any student to choose to consume to buy any school breakfast or lunch to eat from dietary preference program by using prepayment prepaid cost purchase method more easily. Because this prepaid card method will cause these students choose to consume school breakfast or lunch habitually more than every time cash payment method in school.

However, the most successful public health programs are based on an understanding of health behaviour and how which can occur. Therefore, interventions to improve health behaviour can be best designed with an understanding of relevant theories of behaviour change and the ability to use than skill. So, development and implementation and evaluation of public health and health behaviour promotion needs to follow theories and key concepts and summarize the evidence about who use of theory in health behaviour research. A theory is a set of interrelated concepts, definitions that explains or predicts events or situations by specifying relations among variables. Theories can guide the health behaviour research to understand why people do or do not practize health promoting behaviours, helping identify what information is need to design and effective intervention strategy and providing insight into how to design a health behaviour program. It has two types of theory, explanatory theory and change theory. For example, understanding why employee smokes is one step toward a successful effort, but even the least explanations won't e enough by themselves to fully guide change to improve health. Both explanatory and change theories can understand the social determinants of health behaviour. Many social cultural and economic factors contribute to the development, maintenance and change of health behaviour patterns. For another example, employees may bring food with the from home or buy food form workplace, cafeterias and vending machines. Their consumption choices are influenced by personal preferences, habits, nutrition information, availability, cost and placement among other things. The choice process is complex and determined not only by multiple factors, but by factors at multiple. Today, no single theory or conceptual framework dominates research or practice in health promotion and education. For example, lifestyle behaviours, such as sexual risk behaviours and injury prevention, the sexual behavioural players who believe about whether or not who are not at risk for a disease or health problem and their perceptions of the benefits of taking action to avoid it, influence their readiness to take action. So predicting health behaviour changing is needed readiness to change or stage of change has been examined in health behaviour research and found useful in explaining and predicting changes for a variety of behaviours, including smoking, physical activity, e.g. householder families often spend time to drive private car to relax and reduce time to do health sport activities.

Labor economy indicates factors of production uses to create products or services, which are not themselves significantly consumed in the production process. The method to create human capital can be categorized into two types. The first is to utilize human as labor force in the classical economic perspective. It means input of labor force is as other production factors, such as financial capital, land machinery and labor hours. Labor capital includes the reading of human as creator who frames knowledge skills, competency and experience originated by continuously connecting between self and environment. Microeconomic model shows that education investment for workers significantly affects whose productivity in the workplace.

Education can raise to improve workers productivity. Because it is difficult that human capital itself independently contributes to individual development and national economy growth. In fact, it is necessary to link between human capital and economic preference should be considered within a social and political context to precisely measure the human capital. So human capital is one of important factors for a national economic growth. The production oriented perspective of human capital shows to human capital is as a fundamental source of economic productivity.

Many employers prefer to high productive individuals to improve productivity in the internal labor market by the increasing of productivity in the workplace from internal training to raise old or current workers' skill and knowledge in companies. What is labor surplus mean? Labor surplus exists in the sense that a substantial portion of labor force contributes less to output than it requires, i.e. its marginal product falls below surplus designation than arises from the fact that if such workers were reallocated to enhance the total output of the system. For example, agricultural sectors concentrated especially in subsistence agriculture, characterized by family farm, i.e. excluding planation agricultural which consists of profit maximizing, able to hire or fire workers easily. Surplus labor makes its appearance in the owner-operated extended family networks. The company income or output shares are determined via bargaining in relative to through not necessarily equal to the average rather than the marginal product of labor. Large determination is thus based on a sharing principle, a function of the fact that when high man/land rates are part of the initial conditions low marginal productivity workers can't dismissed or otherwise eliminated. Hence, labor surplus phenomenon will raise unemployed and unfair and unreasonable treatment to the job seekers in labor market because employers only concern family relationship business culture and who only feel the old or current workers who have much effort productivity to compare to other job seekers from labor market. I think who are doing unethical behavior not to give chance to employ any other job seekers to fill their internal job positions, due to they only believe their old or current workers working experience and skills must have more effort to be promoted to higher positions in their companies. So, labor surplus economy will raise unemployment ratio and many labor market of proficient and skillful and knowledgeable owned job seekers who can not get more job opportunities if employers only like to do family relationship workplace culture to protect whose current or old labors benefits only. So, these family relationship employers can not raise productivity and also increasing employment ratio in society if who still do not give chance to accept to employ outside job seeker to assist whose business development for long term.

However, labor market policies succeed or fail at least concerning for behavioral response. Insight from behavioral economics, hence consequences for the design and function of labor market policies. For example, the human costs of labor market have rarely been clearer at the value of public policies, such as unemployment insurance and job training programs that assist workers in managing, gaining new skills and navigating the labor of joblessness have been apparent in most major economics in recent years. For the design of unemployment insurance with job search requirements intended to minimize worry to incentives to return to work. I think behavioral economy can apply to labor market finds in these areas to solve labor challenges: unemployment insurance, job search assistance and job training. Hence solving labor moral hazard problems in unemployment compensation schemes of unemployed workers not putting in adequate search efforts and setting inefficiently high reservation wages in response to more generous benefits when unemployed. However, economists have noted several advantages to wage loss insurance, such as the ability to better target benefits to those workers who face the most severe consequence of job loss. Although, behavioral economists doesn't change that logic, it does identify additional advantages to wage loss insurance. There behavioral concerns are consistence with the limited impacts on reemployment rates and job search efforts for encourage the unemployed people have more effort to find new jobs during this period of unemployment period if governments can provide temporary wage loss insurance to them. In any country's labor market, it has supply two sides, the factors affect the decision of an individual. On the supply side, factors include working nature, career path top choose a particular job, requiring education and on the job training, providing effort in particular job. Also, on the demand side, factors that affect the decision of an individual firm factors include: how the firm hires and fires workers, how it offer jobs with different characteristics, how it discriminate among different workers and how it chooses particular compensation policies and to offer different career paths to workers. So, behavioral economist is the combination of psychology and economic that investigates what happens in markets in which some of the agents display human limitations. Does some combination of market formed, learning and evolution these human qualities irrelevant? Because of limits of perfect agents (human) survive and influence what outcomes. Surely, all of economic is meant to be about the behavior of economic agents be whose firms or consumers, suppliers or demanders, bankers or farmers. So what is behavioral economic and how does it differ from other economic? Do only the rational agents survive? Do the workings of markets at least render the actions of rational irrelevant? So, what the decision if it was a mistake to do any rational calculation before the consumer does any decision. So, it seems behavioral economy and psychology has close relationship. It means that human psychology will influence whose decision how to do any economic activities. For example, public economic is the study of how government economic is the study of how government policies influence economic market. Hence, economic analysis is part of the decision making process in any organizations or individuals.

To conclude labor behaviors or performance and consumption behaviors and entrepreneurs environment have different functions to influence any enterprise development to be success . Behavioural economy has close relationship to consumer and employee psychology research. Behavioural economists need to find what causes the consumer why who choose to do whose behaviour or how to predict the consumer avoids to do whose behaviour. Otherwise, labour economists need to concern how to assist the employer to avoid whose employees who feel unfair or unreasonable moral behaviour from whose employer to reduce low productivity caused. Hence, labour economy concerns on individual benefit more than public benefit. Otherwise, behavioural economy concerns on public benefit more than individual benefit. Labour economy concerns on raising individual productivity. Otherwise, behavioural economy concerns on change individual or public habit of behaviour to raise sale.

Bibliography

Roberston, R. (1992), Globalization, Social Theory and

How utility maximization, equilibrium and efficiency concepts influence employee's individual behavior

At the core of behavioral economics is used psychology of economics analysis to improve economics on its own terms generating theoretical insights, making better prediction of field phenomena, and suggesting better policy. It rejects economic theories based on utility maximization, equilibrium and efficiency. It is useful because it provides economists with a theoretical framework that can be applied to almost any form of economic (and even non-economic) behavior.

Simpifying much assumption that are not central to the economic theory. For example, there is nothing in core theory that specifies that people should not care about fairness, that they should weight risky outcomes in a linear fashion, or that they must discount the future at a constant rate. Other assumption simply acknowledge human limits on computational power and self-interest. These assumptions can be considered procedurally rational because human needs to solve problems that are often so complex that who can't be solved exactly by even modern computer technology.

Theories in behavioral economics should be judged by reality, generality and tractability concepts. We share the positivist view that the ultimate test of a theory is the accuracy of its predictions. But we also believe that better predictions are likely to result from theories with more realistic assumptions. In psychology, such as connectionist models that capture some of the essential features of neural functioning, which are based on utility maximization, yet are reaching the point where they are able to predict many judgement and behavioral phenomena. Contrary to the positivistic view, however,

we believe that predictions of feelings.

Most of the ideas in behavioral economics are not new. When economics first became identified as a distinct field of study, psychology didn't exist as a discipline. For example, "invisible hand" and "the wealth of Nations" which belong to theory to moral sentiments, which laid out psychological principles of individual behavior that are arguably as profound as whose economic observations. Another example, such as a simple model of social utility means that one person's utility was affected by another person's payoff. However, the rejection of academic psychology by economists, which constructed an account of economic behavior built up from assumptions about the nature-that is, the psychology of homo-economicus. Nowadays, economists hoped their discipline could be like a natural science. But psychology was not very scientific. The economists thought it provided too unsteady a foundation for economics, who make assumption to utility led to a movement to the psychology from economics. In the early part of the 20th century, economists still included rich speculations about

how people feel and think about economic choices generally. However, later economists are very much appealed to psychological insights, but by the middle of the century discussions of psychology had largely disappeared. Throughout the second half of the century, many criticisms of the positivistic perspective took place in both economics and psychology. The economists of the time had less disagreement with psychology with psychology than they realized. They assume without foundation that behavior always aims at the goal of maximum pleasure and minimum pain; but behavior is not goal-oriented. Also the economists of the time believed false conclusions are drawn from false psychological assumptions. The importance of psychological measures and bounds on rationality. These commentators attracted attention, but did not alter the fundamental direction of economics. One development was the rapid acceptance by economists of the expected utility and discounted utility models which are making decision under uncertainty and choice, respectively. Whereas the assumptions and implications of utility analysis are rather flexible, and the expected utility and discounted utility models have numerous precise and testable implications. As a result, they provided some of the first "hand targets" for critics of the standard theory.

As economists began to accept counterexamples that could be not be permanently ignored, developments in psychology identified promising directions for new theory. Beginning around 1960 year, psychology became dominated by the brain as an information-processing device replacing the behaviorist conception of the brain as a stimulus-response machine. The information-processing permitted a fresh study of neglected topics like memory, problem solving and decision making. These new topics were more obviously relevant to the conception of utility maximization than behaviorism had appeared to be. However, psychologists began to use economic models as a benchmark against which to their psychological models. Early research in behavioral have followed. First, identify assumption or models that are used by economists, who expected utility and discounted utility. Second, the assumption or model is a rule out alternative explanations (such as subjects' confusion or transactions costs). And third, the assumption or model creates alternative theories that generalize existing models. The fourth step is to construct economic models of behavior using the behavioral assumptions to test them from the third step. This final step of economic models of behavior has only been taken more recently to apply.

Costs and benefits analysis concept measures consumer's individual or employee's individual behavior

Entrepreneur needs to know costs and benefits analysis can be applied to predict when consumption behavior will be caused. The methods in behavioral economics are the same as those in other areas of economies. In fact, behavioral economics relied heavily on evidence generated by experiments. More recently, however, behavioral economists have moved beyond experimentation and the full range of methods are employed by economists. The experiment played a large role in the initial phase of behavioral economics because experimental control is exceptionally helpful for distinguishing behavioral explanations from standard ones.

Suppose we observed this phenomenon in these any one of cares, in the form of failures of legal cases to settle before trial, costly divorce proceedings, and labor strikes. They are phenomenons of human' behaviours are caused by costs and benefits measurement of result. Also, behavioural economy would be difficult to tell whether rejection of offers was the result of reputation-building in repeated games, agency problems (between clients and lawyers), confusion, or an expression of distaste for being treated unfairly. However, in these game experiments of failures of legal cases to settle before trial, costly divorce proceedings, and labor strikes. The first three of these explanations are ruled out because the experiments are played once, have no agents, and are simple enough to rule out confusion. Thus, the experimental data clearly establish that subjects are expressing concern for fairness. Other experiments have been useful for testing whether judgment errors which individuals commonly make in psychology experiments also affect prices and quantities in markets. The lab is especially useful for these studies because individual and market-level data can be observed. Although behavioral economists relied on experimental data, however, behavioral economics subject is seen as a very different method from experimental economics. As noted, behavioral economists are methodological profession. They define themselves, not on the basis of the research methods that who employ, but rather their application of psychological insights to economics. Experimental economists, on the other hand, define themselves on the basis of use of experimentation which is as a research tool.

Also, economists have made a major investment in developing experimental methods that are suitable for addressing economic issues, and have achieving among themselves on a number of important issues. For example, experimental economists often make instructions and software available for precise replication, and raw data are typically shared for reanalysis. Experimental economists also insist on paying performance-based. However, experimental economists have also developed rules that many behavioral economists are likely to find excessively . For example, experimental economists rarely collect data like demographics, self-reports, response times and other cognitive measure which behavioral economists have found useful. Descriptions of the experimental environment are usually abstract rather than which are carried on experiment in the outside world because economic theory rarely makes a prediction about how a happen would matter, and experimenters are concerned about losing control over incentives if choosing strategies with certain labels is appealing because of the labels themselves.

Finally, economic experiments also typically use "stationary replication", in which the same task is repeated over and over in each period. Data from the last few periods of the experiment are typically used to draw conclusions about equilibrium behavior outside the lab. When economists believe that examining behavior after it is of great interest, it is also obvious that many important aspects of economic life are like the first few periods of an experiment rather than the last. Supposing if we need to make decision of marriage, educational decisions, and saving for retirement, or the purchase of large durables like houses, sailboats, can cars, which happen just a few times in a person's life, a focus on behavior is clearly not warranted. All said, the focus on psychological realism and economic applicability of research promoted by the behavioral-economics perspective suggests the usefullness research outside the lab and of a broader range of approaches to laboratory research. So, economists realize that who have ideal opportunity to learn by trial-and-error, in a stationary environment, and uses the opportunity to learn how to carry on experimenting any psychology and behavioral researches.

The field of behavioral decision research, on which behavioral economics has drawn more than any other subfield of psychology, typically classifies research into two categories: judgement and choice. Judgement research deals with the processes people use to estimate probabilities. Choice deals with the processes people use to select among actions, considering of any relevant judgements who may have made. Everyday, we need to make probable judgement. Due to judging the likelihood of events is central to economic life. For example: Will you lose your job in a poor economic environment? Will you be able to find another house you like as much as the one you must bid for right away? Will the government raise interest rates? Will a merger strategy increase profits? These questions are answered by some process of judging likelihood. The standard principles used in economic to model probability judgement in economic are concepts of statistical sampling, which are concerned probabilities in the face of new evidence. However, it requires a separation between previously judged probabilities and evaluations of new evidence. However, people often overestimate the probability who previously attached to events which later happened. This leads to "second guessing". For example, Monday morning quarterbacking and may be partly responsible for lawsuits against stockbrokers who lost money for their clients. (The clients think the brokers should have known). For example, anybody has tried to learn from a computer manual has seen the curse of knowledge in action. Another example for making probability judgements is called "representativeness": People judge conditional probabilities like P(hypothesis /data) or P(example/class) by how well the data represents the hypothesis or the example represents the class. Representativeness is an economical shortcut that delivers reasonable judgements with minimal effort in many cases. For example, in judging whether a certain student described in a profile is, say, a psychology major or computer science major, the student decides how well the profile matches the psychology or computer science career to the student generally.

Many studies show how this sort of feature-matching can lead people to under weigh the "base rate", in this example, the overall frequency of the two majors. Another byproduct of representativeness is the "law of small numbers": Small samples are though to represent the properties of the statistical process that generated them (as if the law of large numbers, which guarantees that a large sample of independent draws does represent the process, is in a hurry to work). If a baseball player get hits 30% of his times at bat, but is 0 for 4 , so far in a particular game, then he is "due" for a hit in his next at bat in this game, so that this game's hitting profile will more closely represent his overall ability. Field and experimental studies with basketball shooting and betting on games that people believe that there is positive attitude that players experience the "hot hand", when there is no evidence that such an effect exists. For example, judgements of the fairness or non misleading or reasonable of clients‘ financial report to accounting auditors, consumers buying products and classroom negotiation. It is important to judge whether it is both a good attitude and bad attitude. A good attitude provides fast, close to optimal, answers when time or capabilities are limited, but it also needs logical principles and leads to situations. So, optimal is largely a critique (a reasonable one) of the later applied research. Assume that people misspecify a set of hypotheses, or encode new evidence incorrectly. For example, assuming that people believe hypothesis A is more likely than B will never encode pro-A evidence mistakenly, but will sometimes encode pro-B evidence as being supportive. For another example, investors will think there is wide variation in skill of, say, mutual-fund managers, even if there is no variation at all. (A manager who does well several years is a surprise if performance is mistakenly thought due to non replacement, so concluding that the manager must be really good.)

A question concerns stock market, such as: Overreacts in the long term. In their model, earnings follow a random walk but investors believe, mistakenly, that earnings have positive attitude. After one or two periods of good earnings, the stock market can not be confident that exists and hence expects, but since earnings are really a random walk, the stock market is too pessimistic and is underreacting to good earnings news. After a good earnings, however, the stock market believes many investors are increasing. Since, it is not the stock market is too optimistic and overreact. For another example, valuable consumer products (A $100 wireless keyboard, a fancy computer mouse, bottles of wine, and a box of chocolate) are sold to postgraduate (MBA) business students. The students were presented with a product and asked whether who would buy it for a price equal to the last two digits of their own social security number (a roughly random identification number required to obtain work in the United States) converted into a dollar figure, e.g. , if the last digits were 99, then the postgraduate business students will accept the hypothetical price was $99 to buy any of it for a price to the last two digits of their own social security number . After giving a yes/no response to the question. Would you pay $99? subjects were asked to state the most who would pay (using a procedure that gives people an incentive to say what who really would pay). Although subjects were reminded that the social security number is essentially random, those with high numbers were willing to pay more for the products. However, many studies have also shown that the method used to elicit preferences can have dramatic consequences. Nevertheless, when required to make an economic decisions-to-choose a brand of toothpaste, a car, a job, or how to invest, people do make some kind of decision. Behavioral economists refer to the process by which people make choices with ill defined preferences as "constructing preferences".

However, in classical consumer theory, preferences among different commodities are assumed to be invariant with respect to an individual's current consumption. Specifically, people seem to dislike losing commodities from their consumption much more than they like gaining other commodities. For example, the research of "contingent valuation" studies that attempt to establish the dollar value of products which are not routinely trades. Contingent valuation is often used to do government cost-benefit analysis or establish legal penalties from environment damage. These surveys typically show very large differences between buying prices

(e.g. paying to clean up oil of beaches) and selling prices (e.g. having to be paid to allow beaches to be ruined).

Nowadays, a quarter of the wealth in the USA has more interesting opportunities to do behavioral economies. They find that motivated sellers should regard the price who paid as a sunk cost and choose at a nominal loss from the purchase price. Sellers' listing prices and subsequent selling behavior reflects to nominal losses. There are some cases in which no effect would be expected, such as when products are purchased for resale rather than for utilization. For example, Do art or antique dealers like with pieces who buy to resell? What about surrogate mothers who agree to bear a child for a price paid in advance? However, evidence on the degree of commercial attachment is mixed. Reference points can also serve as social focal points for judging performance. For an interesting example from corporate finance. In general, when managers whose firms face possible losses (or declines from a previous year's earnings) are very reluctant to report small losses. As a result, the distribution of actual losses and gains show a very large at zero, and hardly any small reported losses (compared to the number of small gains). A manager who does not have the skill to shift accounting profits to erase a potential loss (i.e. has some earnings in his pocket.) is considered a poor manager. It seems that the bad performance manager whose behavior is bad to mislead public to believe his firm have better performance in this year. Hence, in the mental accounting view, people set up mental accounts for outcomes which are psychologically separate, much as financial accountants lump expenses and revenues into separated accounts to guide managerial attention. Otherwise, mental accounting stands in opposition to the standard view in economics that it predicts, accurately , that people will spend money coming from different sources in different ways. So, a generalization of the notion of mental accounting is the concept of "choice bracket" , which refers to the fashion in which people make decisions narrowly, in either a piece meal fashion, or boardly, i.e. taking account of interdependencies between decisions. For example, when making many separate choices between products, consumers tend to choose more diversity when the choices are bracketed broadly than when they are bracketed narrowly.

Preferences over risky and uncertain outcomes of individual behavior economic theories.

The expected utility (EU) hypothesis explains that the utility of a risky distribution of outcomes (says, monetary payoffs) is a probability weighted average of the outcome utilities. It follows logically from apparently reasons. Most notably the independence (or " cancellation") choice. The indepence choice says that if you are comparing two gambles, you should cancel events which lead to the same consequence with the same probability, your choice should be independent of those utility also simplifies matters because a person's taste for risky money distributions can be fully captured by the share of the utility function for money.

However, many studies document predictive failures of expected utility in simple situations in which subjects can earn substantial sums of money from their choices. Some of these new theories alter the way in which probabilities are weighted, but preserve a "between" property which says that if A is preferred to B, then any probabilistic gamble between them must be preferred to B, but dispreferred to A (i.e. the gambles like "between" A and B in preference). Other new theories suggest that probability weights are "rank-dependent", outcomes are first ranked, then their probabilities are weighted in a way which is sensitive to how who rank within the gamble that is being considered. For example, if a person is attitude towards gambles really came from the utility of wealth function, even large gains in wealth would not tempt who to risk \$50 or \$100 losses, if who really dislikes losing \$10 more than who likes gaining \$11 at every level of wealth. For example, linear probability weighting in expected utility (EU) works reasonably well except when outcome probabilities are very low or high. But low-probability events are important in the economy in the form of "gambles" with positive (lottery tickets and also risky business ventures in biotechnology and pharmaceuticals) and high risk compensation events which required large insurance industries. Another theory example, such as prospect theory is experimental choices more accurately than (EU) because it gets the psychological of judgement and choice right. It consists of two main components, a probability weighting function, and a "value function" which replaces the utility function of (EU). The weighting function $P(P)$ combines two elements: (1) The level of probability weight is a way of expressing risk tastes (if you hate to gamble, you will place low weight on any chance of winning anything) and (2) $P(P)$ captures how sensitive people are to differences in probabilities.

If people are move sensitive in the neighborhoods of possibility and certainty. i.e. changes in probability near zero and 1, then their $P(P)$ curve will overweight low probabilities and underweight high ones. For another theory example, such as technical motivation for "rank dependent" theories, ranking outcomes, than weighting their probabilities is that when separate probabilities are weighted, it is easy to construct examples in which people will be dominance by choosing a "dominated" gamble A which has a lower chance of winning at each possible outcome amount, compared to the higher chance of winning the same outcome amount for a dominant gamble B. If people rarely choose such dominated gambles, who are acting as if who are weighting the differences in probabilities which is the essence of the rank dependent approaches. So, new information can help any decision maker to feel better to make better decisions. These theories effect may explain demand for information in settings like medicine or personal finance, where new information usually does not change choice, but relieves anxiety people have from knowing there is something who could know but don't. However, the planning problem for economic agents who would like to behave in fashion and discussed the important time discounting for choice. Most big decisions, e.g. savings, educational investments, labor supply, health and diet, crime and drug etc. decisions use have costs and benefits which occur at different point in time. Thus, time discounting is basically standard time discounting plus an immediacy effect, a decision discounts delays in equally at all moments except the current one, caring differently about well being. This functional form provides one sample and powerful model of the taste to individual to make right or reasonable behavior economic decision. However, most analyses of choice assume that people integrate new consumption with planned consumption. It is infeasible and perhaps for this reason, descriptively inaccurate. When people make decisions about new sequences of payments or consumption, they tend to evaluate them in isolation, e.g. treating negative outcomes as losses, rather than as reductions to their existing money flows or consumption plans.

How to decide fairness and social preferences. The assumption that people maximize their own wealth and other personal material goals just self-interest is a correct simplification that is often useful in economics. However, people may sometimes choose to spend their wealth to punish others who have harmed them, reward whose, so who have helped, or to make outcomes more fair. Just as understanding demand for products requires specific utility function, the key to understanding this sort of social preferences is a specification of social utility which can explain many types of date with a single function.

Behavioral economy can also use to assist firms to choose right behavior to decide to do any matters. I show hypothesis to establish any reference level of consumer surplus and product profit. Both sides are entitled to any firm's levels of profit, so price changes which threaten any matter are considered unfair. So raising any product price, it will reduce consumer surplus and is considered unfair. But the cost of a firm's inputs rises, subjects said it was fair to raise prices. Because not raising prices would reduce the firm's profit (compared to the reference profit). Everyday observation that firms don't change prices and wages as frequently commonly. For example, when the fourth Hary Potter story book was released in summer 2000 year, most stores were allocated a small number of books that were pre-sold in advance. Why not raise prices or auction the books off? It is possible that it concerned about customer goodwill and excess demand to cause book stores limit such book price increases. Offended consumers are often able to affect firm behavior by media attention or provoking legislation. For example, scalping tickets for popular sports and entertainment events (resulting them at a large premium over the printed ticket price) is constrained by law in most countries. For example, some countries have "anti-laws" penalizing sellers who take advantage of shortages of water, fuel and other necessities by raising prices after natural disasters. So, the countries' governments can protect which citizen benefits to balance the natural resource supply and demand to sell in the reasonable price fairly after the natural disaster occurrence.

A few years ago, responding to public anger at rising CEO salaries when the economy was being restructured through downsizing and many workers lost their jobs. Otherwise, some countries passed a law prohibiting firms from deducting CEO salaries for tax purposes beyond $1 million a year. because the countries need to earn much tax income from these high salary CEO income every year. So, explaining why these laws and regulations come from is one example of now economics might be used to expand the scope of law and behavioral economic relationship.

What is behavioral game theory?

Game theory has rapidly become an important foundation for many areas of economic theory, such as bargaining in decentralized markets, contracting and organizational structure. The descriptive accuracy of game theory in these application can be questioned because equilibrium predictions often assume strategic reasoning and direct field tests are difficult. In fact, behavioral game theory uses any experimental evidence and psychological research to generalize the standard assumptions of game theory. One component of behavioral game theory is a theory of social preferences for allocations of money to oneself and others. Another component is a theory of how people choose in one shot games or in the first period of a repeated game. For example, in share buying and selling market, shareholders shall buy or sell shares from their judgement in the economic cycle market everyday. So share investment is seemed as allocation of game to these shareholders. Also, shareholders whose mind can influence whose psychological behavior to decide how to invest whose shares in their share investment economic activities. The component of behavioral game theory can include a model of learning to either individual or a population. Also, game theory is one area of economy in which serious attention has been paid to the process by which can equilibrium comes about. Many learning theories have been proposed and carefully tested with experimental data. Theories about population never predict as well as theories of individual learning through who are useful for other purposes. So, behavioral game theory can be applied to these complex environments. e.g. consumer supermarket purchase, share market etc. How to apply behavioral game theory to macroeconomics and saving aspect?

Many concepts in macroeconomic probably have a behavioral style that could be influenced by research in psychology. For example, it is common to assume that prices and wages are in nominal terms, which has important implications for macroeconomic behavoir. Behavioral economics suggests some ideas for among consumers and workers, perhaps it is influenced by workers' concern for fairness. An important model in macroeconomics is the life cycle model of savings or permanent income hypothesis. This theory assumes that people make a guess about their lifetime earnings profile, and plan their lifetime earnings profile, and plan their savings and consumption in each period has diminishing marginal utility; and preferences for consumptions streams are time-separable (i.e. overall utility is the sum of the discounted utility of consumption in each separate period). The theory also assumes people lump together different types income when they guess how much money who will have (i.e. different sources of wealth are different). So, why many young people won't spend too much money for unnecessary expenditure, e.g. entertainment easily. Because who plan to save for their retirement in the future.

A behavioral life cycle theory of savings in which different sources of income are kept track of in different mental accounts. Mental accounts can reflect natural perceptual or cogitive divisions. For example, it is possible to add up the travelever paycheck and dollar value of whose frequent flyer miles, but it is simply unnatural to do so. It is important to note that many key implications of the life-cycle hypothesis have never been well supported (e.g. consumption is far more closely related to current income than it should be according to theory. However, predictions can be improved by introducing utility functions with habit formation in which utility in a current depends on the reference point of previous consumption, and by more carefully accounting for uncertain about future income. So, mental accounting is only one of several behavioral approaches that may prove useful. Economics is money illusion, it is the tendency to make decisions based on nominal quantities rather than converting those figures into real terms by adjusting for inflation. Money illusion seems to be pervasive in some domains. So, it appears that employees don't seem to mind if their real wage falls as long as their nominal wages doesn't fall. Labor macroeconomics is involuntary unemployment. Why can some people not find work beyond of switching jobs, or a natural rate of unemployment? A popular account of unemployment pushs that wages are deliberately paid above the market clearly level, which creates an excess supply of workers and hence unemployment. But why are wages too high ? As efficiency wage theory shows that paying workers more than who deserve is necessary to ensure that who have something to lose if they are unemployed, which motivates them to work hand and economizes on monitoring. Another viewpoint indicates that employer and worker is such as into a gift exchange relationship. Employers pay more than who have to as a gift and workers repay the gift by working harder than necessary. They show how gift exchange can be an equilibrium and show some of its macroeconomic implications. In labor economics, gift exchange is clearly evident of experimental labor markets. In practical working environment, firms offer wages; workers who take the jobs than choose a level of effort, which is costly to the workers and valuable to the firms. For example, firms and workers can enforce wages, but not effort levels. Since workers and firms are matched for just one period, and do not learn each other's identities, there is no way for either side to build reputations or for firms to punish workers who chose low effort. However, self interested workers should shirk, and firms should anticipate that and pay a low wage.

In fact, firms deliberately pay high wages as gifts and workers choose higher effort levels when they take higher wage jobs. It seems that it has strong relationship between wages and effort is stable over time. For example, standard life-cycle theory assumes that if people can borrow they should prefer wage profiles which maximize the present value of lifetime wages. Holding total wage payments constant, and assuming a positive real rate of interest, present value maximization implies that workers should prefer declining wage profiles over increasing ones. However, in fact, most wages profiles are clearly rising over time which is such as a phenomenon. Rather, workers derive utility from positive changes in consumption, but have self-control problems. That would prevent them from positive changes in consumption, but have self-control problems that would prevent them from saving for later consumption of wages were more front-loaded in the life cycle. In addition, workers seem to derive positive utility from increasing wage profiles, it is perhaps because rising wages are a source of self-esteem and the desire for increasing payments is much weaker for non wage income. The standard life-cycle of labor supply also implies that workers should substitute labor and leisure based on the wage rate who face and the value who place on leisure at different points in time. If wage fluctuations are temporary workers should work long hours when wages are high and short hours when wages are low. However, because changes in wages are often persisting and because work hours are generally fixed in the short-run. So, it is difficult to tell whether workers are substituting. For example, taxi drivers who target daily will drive longer hours on low income days early on high income days. This behavior is exactly the opposite of substitution. Also inexperienced taxi drivers support the daily targeting prediction. But experienced taxi drivers don't have negative elastic, either because target minded drivers earn less and self select or taxi drivers learn over time to substitute rather than target. Perhaps the simplest prediction of labor economics is that the supply of labor should be upward sloping in response to a increase in wage.

In finance, standard equilibrium models of asset pricing assume that investors only care about asset risks if who affect marginal publicly available information to forecast stock returns as accurately as possible the efficient markets hypothesis. When those hypotheses do make some accurate predictions and some investors in assets have limited rationality of behavioral finance. Also, in share stock market, it is common, shareholders should not want to trade with them, but the volume of stock market transaction is large. So, it presents data on individual trading behavior which suggests that the extremely high volume may be driven, in part, by overconfidence on the part of investors. For example, property agent's individual behavior is similar to share agent's individual behavior. In the economy view, property agent bases a list price for a house on the selling prices of nearly houses that is similar ("comparables"). Every nearest neighbour techniques bases on similarity is also used in credit scoring and other kinds of evaluations. Also, one firm whose every share sale on the selling price is comparable to its similar firms whose every share price in its same business industry. The shareholder will evaluate whose every share issued sale price in the stock (share) market. Otherwise, in behavioral economy view, for example, property or share buyer who has risky choice to decide to buy in the property or share market. It is a process of comparing the similarity of the probabilities and outcomes in two gambles and choosing on dimensions which are dissimilar.

As we mentioned above, behavioral economics simply includes an interest in psychology. In fact, we believe that many familiar economic distinctions do have a lot of behavioral content, they are implicitly behavioral, and could surely benefit from more explicit ties to psychological ideas and data. However, some people do not feel psychology and economy which have close relationship. Such as, substantial debate is ongoing in psychology about whether knowing the precise details of how the brain carries out computations is necessary to understand functions and mechanisms of driving car skill at higher levels, (knowing the mechanical details of how a car works may not be necessary to turn the key and drive it). Most psychology experiments use indirect measures like response times, error self reports and natural experiments, due to brain has been fairly successful in codifying what we know about thinking, but pressimists think brain scan studies won't add much. The optimists think the new tools will lead to some discoveries. Another couple is the distinction between short run and long run price elasticity which concerns behavioral economy. In fact, economy needs have theories concepts to support any evidence to prove any matter has happened. Concerning short run and long run price elasticity cause and effort issue, with a casual suggestion that the run is the time it takes for markets to adjust, or for consumers to learn new prices, after a demand or supply stock. Adjustment costs undoubtedly have technical and social component, but probably also have some behavioral factors influence in the form of gradual adaption to loss and learning.

Another macroeconomic model which can be interpreted as implicitly behavioral is that business cycles can emerge if it is not general price inflation, so why the consumers shall not decide to buy this kind of product in the competitive market. For example, risky choice is as a process of comparing the similarity of the probabilities and outcomes in two gambles, and choosing on dimensions which are dissimilar. Behavioral economic simply includes an interest in psychology. In fact, we believe that many familiar economic distinctions do have a lot of behavioral content, they are implicitly behavioral and could surely benefit from more explicit ties to psychological ideas and data. However, some people do not feel psychology and economy which have close relationship. Such as psychology is about whether knowing the precise details of how the brain carries out computations is necessary to understand functions and mechanisms at higher levels. (knowing the mechanical details of how a car works may not necessary to turn the key and drive it.) Most psychology experiments use indirect measures like response times, error rates, self reports and natural experiments due to brain has been fairly successful in codifying what we know about thinking. However, pessimists think brain scan studies won't add much. The optimists think the new tools will lead to some discoveries and the potential is great that they cannot be ignored. However, economy needs have theories or concepts to support evidence to prove why any matters had happened. An example, is the distinction between short term and long term price elasticity. This distinction, mentions between of them, with a casual suggestion that long run is the time it takes for markets to adjust, or for consumers to learn new prices, after a demand or supply shock. Adjustment costs undoubtedly have technical and social components, but probably also have some behavioral factors influence in the form of gradual adaption to loss and learning.

However, organizational behavioral theory concerns that organizatonal contracting are shot through with implicitly behavioral economics. Some economists motivate the incompleteness of contracts as a consequence of rationality in foreseeing the future, but do not tie the research directly to work on memory and imagination. For example, agency theory begins with the presumption that there is some activity the agent doesn't like to do. Why markets are better at making dramatic changes than managers influence cost. So, influence costs are the costs managers preform for projects who like or personally benefit from like promotion or raises. A lot of influence costs are undoubtedly inflated by optimistic, each division manager really does think their division desperately needs funds and social comparison of pay and benefits. Otherwise, why are salaries kept so secret? In all these cases, conventional economic behavior has deeper psychological questions of where adjustment costs, effort and influence costs come from. So, it beings these questions: Could these phenomena surely produce surprising testable prediction? Is psychology regularity an assumption or a conclusion?

Behavioral economics generally begins with assumption rooted in psychological regularity and asks what follows from those assumptions. An alternative approach is to work backward, regarding a psychological regularity as a conclusion that must be proved an explanation that must be derived from deeper assumption before we fully understand and accept it. The alternative approach is caused by a fashionable new direction in economic theory and psychology too, which is to explain human behavior as the product of evolution. However, we may not believe that behavior of intelligent, modern people lived in socialization and cultural influence can only be understood by guessing what their lives were like and how their brains might have adapted generally. There are other models that treat psychological regularity as a conclusion to be proved rather than an assumption to be used. Such models usually begin with an observed regularity. Economists have for deriving behavior from first principles and rationalizing apparent irrationality. Theories of this sort are useful behavioral economics and what fresh predictions do they make. However, critics have pointed out that behavioral economics is not a unified theory, but is instead a collection of tools and ideas.

This is true. However, some economists believe that economic models do not derive much predictive power from the single tool of utility maximization. The goal of behavioral economic is to develop better tools that, in some cases, can do both jobs at once. Economists like to point out the natural division of labor between scientific disciplines: Psychologists should concern to individual minds, and economists to behavior in games, markets, and economies. But the division of labor is only efficient if there is effective coordination, and all too often economists fail to conduct intellectual trade with those who have a comparative advantage in understanding individual human behavior. The only question is whether the implicit psychology in economics is good psychology or bad psychology. We think it is simply unwise, and inefficient to do economics without paying some attention to good psychology.

How entrepreneur applys behavioral economic strategy to do decision

Behavioral economics theories can also apply to assist any policy makers to make right and reasonable decision in right time. I shall indicate new principles to recommend and I also shall give any psychological cases to explain how policy makers can apply behavioral economic theories to judge how to make their any decision is the most right and the most reasonable.

Behavioral economy is an independent and demonstrates real economic well-being. It aims to improve quality of life by promoting innovative solutions that challenge mainstream thinking on economic, environment and social issues. Also, behavioral economy is different branches of more alternative economies into a form that is useful primarily for policy-makers. I think behavioral economy can be given an aid to policy makers how who use economic tools to the broader policy making community by providing a theoretical behaviour for many policy approaches to be used. The standard economic analysis assumes that humans are rational and behave in a way to maximize their individual self-interest. This rational man assumption indicates a powerful tool for analysis. However, it has many shortfalls that can lead to unrealistic economic analysis and policy-making. Also, I think behavioral economics and psychology has these principles to influence human behaviour. These principles include, such as below:

In common, people do many things by observing others and copying; people are encouraged to continue to do things when they feel other people approve of their behaviour. People do many things without consciously thinking about time. These habits are hard to change. There are cases where money is de-motivating as it undermines people's intrinsic motivation. People want their actions and commitments to be values usually. People put undue weight on recent events and who cann't calculate probabilities well and worry too much about unlikely events and who are strongly influences by how the problem/information is presented to them. People need to feel effective to make a change, even just giving who the incentives and information is not necessarily enough in any environment usually. So policy makers ought concern about these human behavior principles to judge whose behaviors are right or wrong, then who can decide to do any economic activities more reasonable, e.g. decisions of consumption, policies making, investment etc.

In fact, much of our behaviour is strongly influenced by other people's behaviour. Social learning is a process by which we take in the behavior of others to learn how to behave. In more complex situations with which we are unfamiliar, we consciously watch and learn from the behavior of others. For example, when use a new library for the first time. When we mist make a conscious decision on how to behave, our sense of social identity is important, we think: how would other from my group behave in this situation? In situations where there is high social capital. i.e. where there are strong networks between people and a high level of mutual trust, so its seems other people's behaviour and our sense of social identity may be extremely important in influencing our own behavior and policy makers ought need to know how to judge their behaviour whether their behavior is either right and reasonable or wrong and unreasonabe in any learning process of environment. The standard economic theory is tried to explain where people's preferences come from, so it does not take account of the direct influence of the people's behaviour and social norms on our behaviour. The theory assumes we independently know what we want and that our preferences are fixed. This standard theory is very good at explaining short-term decision making. For example, I want green vegetables and choose fruits as they are on special offer, but it cannot explain longer term changes in preferences. I now only choose organic food. Along the same lines the importance of institutions, such as regulations, for example, how people organise markets and the evolution of the whole economi system are not subjects of general economic analysis. This has significant implications for policy design.

In fact, the standard economic theory also assumes that people carry out a full rational analysis of all consumers' available options. This is not what we do; we often just copy the actions of other people. For example, it would require too much effort to look up all the rules when driving in a new country, to find out all the fines/punishments for failing to meet the rules, to work out the probability of being caught and the possible costs, before deciding how to drive there. Instead we just copy other people, and perhaps adjust our behaviour according to the feedback we receive. However, some psychologists indicate to see people how to behave, especically in crises situations and when others are experts. These psychologists have identified that we are open to influence from people in authority or people we like. When we are influenced by authority, an expert, someone with legitimate power to direct our actions, someone who can either reward or punish us. The effects are less likely to be lasting than we are influenced by someone we like.

However, some people's psychological behaviour is similar to economic behaviour to judge to make any decision. For example, why do you wear a seatbelt in your car? Most of us wear seatbelts as it has become normal behaviour, everyone does it. We neither evaluate the likelihood of having an accident, nor the chance of getting caught without our seatbelt on and incurring a fine. The enforcement of seatbelt wearing is now hardly necessary, as it has become a social norm. What does this mean for policy makers? Policy makers focusing only on economic analysis may often devise a system that has an immediate effect. In psychologists view this issue point, knowing that there is a fine for speeding and a high likelihood of getting caught, the driver will probably drive more slowly, but who will drive just as fast one who realise the chance of being caught is low. However, of policy makers can change the social norm, perhaps in this case by encouraging us to frown on others who drive dangerously fast with campaigns against dangerous driving, then less enforcement will be needed after the change. In other words policy makers might want to take preferences as fixed in the short term, but they should consider shifting preferences in the medium term. An example where policy appears to have successfully changes people's preferences in the US and Singapre and Hong Kong is banning smoking in public places. This change appears to reduce the social proof of the amount people smoke in private places and public places both also. It seems that government policies can influence the decreasing numbers of consumers require to buy cigeratte to smoke habitually, due to fine and punishment is regulated to be ban effectively. Such daily routines quickly became habits. Even when we consciously think about what we do, it can be difficult to change our behaviour. Perhaps I think it is a good idea for people to use public transport, but I do not know where the bus stop is or when the bus runs. I think to use private car to drive to work place is more preference choice. The reward feeling , my journey by car was easy and free to reinforce my old bad habit. Psychologists theories on changing habits generally involve raising it to a conscious level where we can consider the merits of alternative behaviour. This is followed by adopting the new behaviour, which, with time, becomes frozen as a new habit. Thus, I think that we need have regulation to control my behaviour, then we can change my behaviour to be new habit from old habit of behaviour easily. For example, human blood sale is an economic product, due to paying donors for blood would increase supply. Supplies would be provided at a cost advantage in the future, if demand continued to rise. Such as supplies to hospitals for blood will has cost from donors when there are many patients need much blood to use to treat any diseases in any hospitals. Otherwise, if there are not many patients need much blood to use, but there are many donors have effort to provide blood to any hospitals, then it will be economic inefficiency and it is highly wasteful of blood. Thus, the blood donors whose blood supplies of behavior and the cost of blood which will concern to the hospitals patients' numbers of demand, so their behavior and economy has close relationship in the hospital blood demand market.

For shareholder behaviour example, if you hold some shares in a firm that has gone down in value. What do you do? Many people hold on to their shares in this situation, in the hope that they will recoup their losses. Conversely, when shares have gone up in share, people are happy to sell them to realise their gain, A similiar behaviour is also observed for professional traders who tend to hold on to shares with a loss for longer than those with a gain. The traders who exhibit this type of loss to a lesser degree tend to be the more successful ones.

For another example, this is a case where the theory is directly applicable within economic cost-benefit-type analyses that include valuations of no-market products, such as valuations of pollution damage. Policy makers have a choice as to whether-to-accept, and as these may vary by up to a factor, the outcome of such an analysis many well depend on which value is chosen. When a policy maker reasonably has a right to something that might be taken away from them, the willing-to-accept value would be used. On the other hand, when the policy maker only reasonable has a right to the status quo and an improvement is proposed, then the willingness-to-pay is the correct value to use.

What behavioral economic preferences regarding time discounting theory would pay and the conclude that the discounted psychologists have long established utility model, which continues to be that people don't make decisions in widely used by economists, has little the way assumed. In generaly, people are expected to rationally make the best choices given their preferences, independent of how these choices are presented. Therefor more information and choice is always considered good. Using this theory, policy makers should ensure that people always have as much information and as many things to choose between as possible, the process of introducing policy is irrelevant. Ideas from behavioural economic indicate, however that this is not the right approach.

However, we know from experimental economics that more choice and more information can lead to a feeling of helplessness or reduced self-efficiency. Hence, if people hope have better solutions to a probem. Instead, providing people with opportunities for inderstanding, exploration and participation engages powerful motivations for competence, being needed. In summary, people 's self-efficacy increases and they are motivated toward implementing the solutions. i.e. changing their behaviour in a desired way. So, a participatory approach not only improves policy, it also makes to any policy makers more happier. In most cases these principles cannot be used directly as part of any mathematical economics analysis, but highlight situations where this standard analysis will not accurately describe human behaviour and therefore might have unintended consequences when implemented in policy. However, that the policy implications could be quite powerful as the behavioural approach provides quite different lines of analysis to the standard economic model. It is heartening to see policy makers focusing more on the psychology of behaviour when devising policy. So behavioral economics is a relatively new field of economics that attempts to incorporate insights from psychology into economic models and analyses. As above cases seem any policy maker's economic activites which are relative to whose psychology's decision. However, psychologists are often interest in understanding at the level of individual or social group of behaviour, the primary interest in economic is usually in understanding how behaviour and interactions play out in a system to shape economic outcomes. Economists are interested in system-level outcomes, such as the level and path of wages, the effect of taxes on economic output, how rates of savings respond to interest rates etc. However, those economic outcomes depend on complex interactions of individuals. So, behavioural economy concerns to how to judge individual to do the reasonable or right behaviour to hope to get the reasonable economic result as well as it's goal rather to help improve any policy makers to understand their behaviour in ways that allow economists to make better predictions and suggest better economic policies. However, new elements about information processing or individual preferences might impact economic models and analyses.

Is psychology influencing all field of economics? It is possible that behavioral economy needs theoretical contributions and laboratory evidence to support to make any reasonable or right decision to any policy makers. This type of work generally uses existing observational data and estimates relationships between variables of interest by either using naturally occurring variation in the data i.e. natural experiment.

Perhaps more than any other field, behavioral economics has had a large impact on finance to the point that behavior finance is often considered a separate field as opposed to being of behavioral economics. Also, public economic is the study of how government policies in fluence economic markets. A primary emphasis of public economic involves the topic of taxation. Otherwise, the biggest impact that the behavioral approach has had in economic is the analysis of retirement saving to influence any employees' decisions about their retirement savings. However, when employees can do make any active savings choices to prepare their retirement. If employers can assist whose employees to design any methods to allocate fund, then accumuates interest and is tax free until the retirement funds are withdrawn to every retirement employee. The tax advantage make effort to save for retirement.

Behavioral economic is in understanding how individuals do or do not smooth consumption over time. Smoothing consumption is a standard economic models. It suggests that individuals should borrow or save in order to consume a similar amount throughout one's lifetime. For example, a teacher who is paid a salary 12 months a year, who should not spend all whose salary within one year. Rather, the teacher should smooth whose consumption over the 12 month period. How to allocate to spend paychecks, food and social security payments which concerns the teacher decide to spend whose salary efficiently. Hence, who needs to plan how he shall spend whose one year salary to be reasonable use in the future. Public economic is to understand how people respond to taxation and social benefit programs. This has been an area that has seen an explosion of behavioral work in recent year. i.e. how taxpayers can experience over-withholding and receive tax refunds from tax department.

Policymakers and insurers are also increasingly turning to psychology for approaches to improve health behavior. Traditionally health-policy focused largely on information provision, assuming that as long as individuals were well informed, their decisions would maximize their health choices. Influential work on the effects of smoking taxes, however, well being of smokers appears to increase with higher taxes to influence health behaviours are not completely rational.

Behavioral economic has also had a small impact on the study of criminal behaviour. For example, individuals are not less likely to commit a crime when who are 18 age and the pubishment of doing so increases dramatically. However, some economists explain the motivations people have for giving to charity and who understand the psychological motivations for charitable giving. So, it seems that charity award giving has probable to reduce 18 age people who choose to do crime behaviour easily because who feel who have effort to assist charity in their life time.

Industrial organization economists study why firms exist and how which function and compete with each other. Insights and psychology and behavioral economics have made a significant contribution to develop that model the interactions of profit maximizing firms with their customers. In fact, firms often need to evaluate whether their products if prices are needed to set what of price of level is the most reasonable and attractive to customers to choose to buy their products. For example, individuals choose cell phone plans with fixed minute allotments and steep charges for going over the minute limits, but frequently exceed their plan limits. This behavior is the best explained by a model in which people overestimate the precision of their demand forecasts. So, cell phone firms need to research how cell phone plans with fixed minute allotments ans steep charges of cell phone call fee charge plan is the most acceptance method to cell phone clients generally. However, cell phone call charge plan and various cell phone product features and the way cell phone clients allocate their limited attention affects cell phone products markets which are external important factors can influence any cell phone clients why who will choose to use the cell phone call plan because any cell phone will be very large durable product to any cell phone consumer after who choose to buy the cell phone product. Hence, who will not often choose to use the old cell phone firm call charge plan if who feel it provides the excellent cell phone call service and reasonable phone call plan to use to compare other cell phone call plans in the cell phone call market. Hence, the cell phone call firm needs to research why consumers need to choose to use which cell phone call plan among of other cell phone call plans in the cell phone call market. Also, researching the cell phone buyers' choice behaviour why who choose to buy the cell phone to use issue, which will have influence to the cell phone buyer why who choose to use the cell phone call charge plan because expensive cell phone is needed to use excellent quality of cell phone call service usually. Otherwise, cheap cell phone is needed to use poor quality of cell phone call service usually. So, cell phone call plan is needed to follow the cell phone quality and price to be used and they ought have direct relationship to influence why the cell phone buyer who chooses to use the cell phone call plan.

Finally, behavioral economic can also apply to be used to labor supply as a motivating in negative or positive labor supply elasticities example. For example, it is possible that taxi drivers work fewer hours when wages are high-consistent with a model of daily income targeting. This finding is that when wages are high (perhaps it is raining and thus it is easy to find people who want a taxi ride), taxi drivers are able to hit their daily target quickly and then go home. However, when wages are low, taxi drivers are not able to hit their target quickly and thus work additional hours in order to hit their target. It means taxi driver's behaviour produce the effect that taxi driver works more when wages are low than when wagers are high. This work has resulted to analyze taxi driver of labor supply decisions with daily reference points in non taxi domains. So, instead of the weather and client numbers and taxi charge factors, the factors of taxi drivers' hours worked and the quality of service is produced is another important factor to influence any taxi drivers' numbers to supply to the taxi market.

Behavioral economic has also influenced the understanding of how staffs can impact worker productivity and job satisfaction. For example, it is possible that poor cooperation can cause worker productivity decreases and it can also cause poor job satisfaction to the worker. So, when working environment can impact productivity, social comparisons can have an impact on job satisfaction as well as the worker's job satisfaction and search intentions are affected by knowing about the salaries of their peers in whose firm. Hence, the worker's positive or negative psychological feeling to whose employers which will have effort to influence whose working performance and productivity to whose firm in possible.

Behavioral economic is increasingly being used in the field of development economics or low income countries. Such as, how Philippines can offer commitment to individuals who wanted to save money in whose country or how Philippines can change to smoking behaviour when commitment devices were offered to Philippine smokers. So, Philippines policy makers need to concern resource scarcity and resource allocation issue to solve how to let its low income level householders can raise to the middle income level to achieve the high income level householders and the low income level householders whose income level is not distant very much.

Why does consumer psychology and economy environment has clos relationship

Entrepreneurs need to understand consumer psychology and economy environment has close relationship. Finally, I shall analyze whether the relationship between the discipline of behavioral economy and psychology which two branches are totally opposite or if the behavioral theories are only complement that mainstream economics.

I think study of economics is the behavior of the complex human beings; this science examines how people choose to act and allocate resources in different market situations. So the economic analysis, is based on the implications that arise from a series of simple assumptions (which are sometimes cited as unrealistic) regarding the human nature. However, in psychological view, the individual is characterized by unlimited rationality and by the ability to follow time consistent, in every situation, his self-interest. In these conditions, behavioral economic attempts to consider a field of analysis in the study of economic phenomena. Because economics deals with the study of human behaviour on the market, it highlights the human character of the science and the fact that, besides of all the patterns and models, the analysis refers to the real individual. It is also behavioural because it attempts to combine approaches from several sciences mainly from economics and psychology, and also from sociology, philosophy, anthropology or biology. This is not an easy mission, in the conditions in which these various disciplines have adopted in time different approaches that became, in many ways, contradictory. So, behavioural economics is that a multidisciplinary appraoch will increase the explanatory power of economics.

On one hand, there are specialists two argue that behavioural economic is a field of economics that continues the hand, there are others who see it as a distinctive school of thought, which proposes a new paradigm. However, behavioural economists propose a multidisciplinary study, criticize certain assumptions on which the traditional model is built (such as rationality and self-interest, in their unlimited form), resource to experiments (the classical method of psychology) to validate some assumptions, propose new theories (such as the prospect theory) and advance different interpretations of the economic behaviour, e.g. how to maximize consumers satisfy their needs. This issue is concerned to concern consumption of pshchology and social economic situation research aspect.

Also, I think that behavioural economics can help the economic science by describing more realistically the utility functions of the individuals. This field of study is based rather it is a natural extension of the basic approach. However, it is can be claimed that behavioural economics is also built on the premise that psychology methods and assumptions are equally important. Also, models of behavioural economics, allow the utility to depend on the differences between one's own level and a reference level. People are sensitive to changes and preferences are not stable in time. The vision of behavioural economics concerning the inter-temporal choice (which assumes that individuals prefer immediate gains and delay unpleasant activities) seems to be more appropriate to the human behaviour that the one of the traditional model (which assumes that utility is updated over time).

In conclusion, I shall indicate two theories to explain why economy and psychology has close relationship to influence human do any behavioural economic activities daily. For example, through the prospect theory, behavioural economics adds new parameters to improve the mathematical modelling method, which was advanced by economists for decisions taken under uncertainty. However, the theory also proposes a slightly different interpretation. The results are interpreted by the individual as positive or negative deviations from a reference point, which has a neutral psychological value.

Last but not least, in addressing social preferences, behavioural economics adds parameters that increase the concern of decision-makers to also assess their utility function in relation to others. For another example, the choice theory; secondly there is not a common consensus between the specialists of behavioural economics regarding the variables that should be included; and finally, many variables that affect the behaviour are not quantitative, but qualitative, and cannot be precisely measured. The findings of behavioural economic are relevant and can help the mainstream theory by providing a more realistically base of study. However, this argument has contributed to the development of behavioural economics, because there are a large number of phenomena that cannot be entirely emplained by the mainstream economics. So, why in the beginning, I indicated why behavioural economics does not imply the totally exclusion of the neoclassical approach and the most studies in this area try to provide a more realistic base of the standard theory.

In the concluding, I believe that in time, behavioural economic models will replace the simplified ones, based on unlimited rationality. Also, economists have provided a great importance to the quantitative structures, departing from the human nature. However, behavioural economics can become truly revolutionary only it it will always be receptive and will provide a critical insight to their own theories and perspectives, and especially the ones regarding the aspects that they reproach to the traditional economic theory. However, I also feel that the individual's behaviour on the market is determined only be economic factors. In brief, individual choices and, by this, the demand variation are explained only and the variations in the prices of products/services and the available personal income. Am inportant discussion in the field of determine directly the economic behaviour of an individual (like the sociological and psychological of factors) are actually active elements in the process the reshaping of the utility functions. Finally, in my view, I believe that the conduct of the market phenomena, as it occurs in reality. In this sense, the research of behavioural economics aims to see how the neoclassical model could be improved, using mainly psychology concepts. Although, there are some specialists who argue that behavioural economics can be an alternative to the neoclassical theory.

Most findings, of my study conducted in this book, modify some of standard economical assumptions, in order to provide a greater psychological realism. However, the additions proposed by behavioural economists simply recognize the human limitations on (mentally) calculations, will and self-interest. So, I think psychology and economy has close relationship to influence any policy makers or decision makers to do any economic psychology daily. Because the purpose of economics is to better understand and explain the conduct of the economic activities as which occur in reality. Otherwise, human being is complex and its behaviour and constitution is studied by all the social sciences. Consequently, multi and interdisciplinary approaches can bring real benefits to the economic science, by providing a more realist foundation to cause any policy makers or decision makers how to decide to make any behaviours or economic activities by behavioural economic activities support daily.

FOUR

WHY SOCIAL BEHAVIOR MAY INFLUENCE ORGANIZATIONAL STRATEGY NEEDS TO BE CHANGED

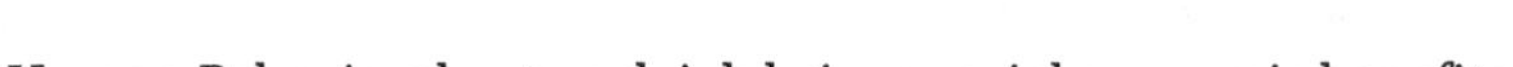

Human Behavioral network job brings social economic benefits

What does human network job mean ? Why may human network job be popular? Why human network job behavior may influence economy ?
Nowadays internet is popular to use. We can apply internet to find data , search any new things, even earn money. Why does internet
may become huma network job source. For example, e-publish may be one kind of new human network job. Any authors may apply internet
channel to help them to sell electronic or paper books from e-publisher web store. They may apply facebook, you tub etc. any online
channel to promote themselves new books to let new readers to know whether when they may buy themselves favourable new topic books to read from electronic publisher web store.

Thus, future electronic publisher industry may help any authors to build internet network platform to help them to sell and promote
ot advertise their any one new electronic or paper book topic to let global any one reader to choose to buy their any new topic books from electronic publisher web store easily and conveniently. However, it implies that electronic network platform author may be one kind of future new human network job in our societies.

How electronic network platform author job may bring economy benefit in macro economy view? A person can have few friends, contacts and still be very influential if these few
friends and contacts are themselves highly influential, e.g. one author must not need to know any one reader in global society. When they like to choose any electronic books from electronic internet network platform. They may become the author's any one topic book buyer, when they feel the author's any one topic book is fun and attract they make decision to buth the strange author whose the topic book from electronic book publisher's platform web store conventiently in short time. Although, they are strangers, they do not know themselves , but the reader can understand what it way that made Google from writing platofrm to create new creative mind and typing network job method to replace traditional hand writing book method for global authors. It will be one kind of new human network writing job.

Hence, global any one reader can apply an innovative search engine , such as google.com to find whether whom author personal new topic books are value to read from internet.
Then, the electroniuc publisher's web store may be new book store platform sale network to help the author to sell many electronic or paper books from electronic network platform
in short time. So, internet may be future new network plaform to help global any one author to create network writing job absolutely. Furthermore, internet may be popular social media
to help any one author to build goold relationship between his/her readers. It is one kind of new network, human network job. New authors do not need to buy many paper books to prepare to put in any one book shop warehouse. Their every book can print on demand to reduce out of book stock in any one book shop. They may choose to sell either electronic books or paper books both from any one book publisher web store. So, electronic network platform may be one kind of good writing channel to help human authors to create income and it can also help authors to bring new creative mind and

new topic fun content books to let readers to know and buy to read from electronic publisher network platform.

Why does human behavior may be one kind of new human network job to bring global economic advantages. ALthough, it may be free income or without inocme, but the person does the network behavior, his/her behavior may be bring advantages to influence many other people's health. For this case, when a worker in a coffee shop in an airport gets a vaccination aganinst the flu, it does not only helps him or her stay healthy, but also helps the many travellers who might otherwise have been inflected if that workers caught the flu. So, the externality , the result implies the vaccination of even a part of a community conveys benefits to the whole community. For example, governments pay special attention to the vaccinations of school children, teachers, health mothers, and the elderly, categories of people particularly susceptible not only to catching, but also to transmitting a disease.

It is not accidental that governments are heavily involved with vaccination . When there are externalities, free market, fail to persuade individual incentives with society's
their the worker's decision of whether to get a vaccine ends up attracting whether other people get sick. The workers might not fully take all these other people's potential suffering into account when making her or his vaccination decision.

As Stanford University does many suggestions, understand this and tries to help them make the right decisions and so providers free flu vaccines for its staff and students.
Small pockets of unvaccinated individuals can allow a disease to gain a spread more widely well-being. For example, parent weighing the costs and benefits of a vaccine for their child is not always thinking of the consequences of that vaccination to other people. THese are markets in which subsidizing or regulating behavior can make everyone better off. Because the reason for requiring that a child be vaccinated before enrolling in school is not just to protect that child, because each child's vaccination affects others via potential contagions.

Robots take our jobs behavioral and economy influences

Robot job behavior brings economy influences

If one day robots can replace human to do simple, even complex jobs. They will bring what influences to our global societial economy.The popular

economic refrain declares that the
global middle class is dying and robots will soon take our jobs, e.g. shopping center customer service jobs, library service jobs, cinema ticket sale jobs, restaurant kitchen cooker jobs,
even, bus drivers, taxi drivers etc. public transport driving jobs, accountant, doctors etc. professional jobs. Whether it is beautiful or petty matter if our future societies have many human jobs can be replaced to do from robots. Businessman must may reduce to employ employees and reduce to pay salary or wage, when robots can be replaced to do their employees tasks. But, societies must bring unemployement rate rises , due to societies will have many people loss jobs when their employers choose to buy robots to serve their clients or do any office tasks or customer service or cleaning etc. tasks.

In micro economy view, employers may save money in long term, but in macro economy view, it will cause unemployment ratio rises , even crime rate rises when there are many people lose
jobs in societies. These models of doom, though, fail to account for the hundreds of businesses riding the waves of change in their industries when robots may be invented to replace human to do many simple , even complex tasks in our future societies.

WE may image that one small factory needs to manufacture fishes canes to sell to supermarket, the small , cheaper stuff and higher margin parts of the fishes manufacture industry. Before, this factory needs to employe many human factory workers need to help every fresh customer makeing the perfect fishing gear, designed for performance, durability, and cost in order to achieve to manufacture every fish cane in whole fished processing manufacturing stages. Every worker needs to spend about 15 to twenty minutes to finish every fish cane , till to delivery to any supermarket to sell. If this fish canes manufacturing factory can apply manufacturing robots to help them to finish any one working tasks , every robot can only spend five minutes to finish whole fresh fish cane manufacturing process. Thus, every robot can
help this factory save 10 to 15 minutes time to finsh every fish cane manufacturing process. IN fact, time is money, because when every robot can help this factory to reduce 10 to 15 minutes time to compare human worker. Then, this factory can finish about 20 fish canes in one hour if it can use robot to help it to manufacture fish canes. Otherwise, if this factory still use human workers to help it to manufacture fish canes, then it can finsh

about 3 to 4 fish canes in one hour. SO, the manufacturing efficiency ensures that robots must help this fish manufacturing factory to raise fish canes number more than human workers. So, in robotic behavioral economy view, manufacturing robots must help this fish canes manufacturing factory to raise fish canes manufacturing number and deliver increasing number to supermarkets to prepare to sell every day. Robots can help this fish canes manufacturing factory bring manufacturing time saving, rising manufacturing efficiency, improving performance and reducing wages expenditure long time advantages in micro economy view. However, manufacturing robots can also bring disadvanages to society, e.g. increasing unemployment ratio, increasing crime rate,
this factory workers will lose jobs and income, they need earn social welfare from government and increasing government finance pressure in short time, even long time in macro economic view.

Stanford University graduate program in economics, Scott lecturer explained that "in demand and supply economic theory for robots supply and demand case, robots supply number increasing may influence human workers demand number decrease. It sometimes calls " the efficient frontier".
No specific human beings were mentioned in any of economics classes. As robots supply and demand in market case, They (robots) may be purely theoretical " agents" who reached to the most reasonable sale prices in order to persuade any one businessman buyer to make manufacturing robot buying decision whether robots can help him / her to bring how much saving time , saving money, saving cost, improving performance, efficiency economic benefit before he/she plans to reduce workers number when he/ she decides to apply robots to replace human workers in his/her factory or office or any service department, e.g. cinema ticket sale service, shopping center customer service, shopping center cleaning , supermarket customer service etc. service or sale tasks. When robots can replace human to do any one of these tasks in any organizations. So, robots may be human worker agents who reached to prices the way robots would react to a software command. There was nothing that explained why some people thrived and others did n't or why truly brilliant, hardworking people could fail when much lazier folks succeeded." Having been admitted to the Stanford University graduate program in economics, Scott lecturer hoped to get his answers there.

How robots influence our future social changing? Using the right technology can be a boon to your business in this economy. For internet example, it is easier than ever to find well-matched customers all around the world, to stay in contact with them, and to more quickly design the products they want. If you focus solely on being cutting -edge, though you risk letting the technology

take over what should be very robust relationships with your customers , employees, and colleagues. IN nowaddays society, technoligical advances and cutomation, personal

relationships in business are more crucial than ever. I mean that robots can not replace human to serve clients to let them to feel more comfortable and passion more easily. For shoe shop case example, if the shoe shop apply one robot to serve its clients to replace human shoe salesperson to serve its shoe customers. Robots ensure that they can not persuade every shoe potential buyer to make shoe buying decision more easily when robots need to contact every shoe potential buyer. The reason is simple, because robots can not touch any one shoe buyer individual emotion very easier.

If the shoe buyer needs the robots to help him/her to choose any right shoe styles when he/she can not feel himself / herself can make the most right shoe style choice decision. The robots can not replace human shoe salesperson to make shoe style choice judgement more easily. They must need longer time to analyze whether which shoe style may be the most suitable to the shoe buyer. Otherwise, human shoe salesperson may attempt to make the most right shoe style choice decision to help any one shoe buyer to chooce the most right style shoe because he/she owns shoe style sale experience, shoe style knowledge, the most important reason is that they can feel every shoe customer individual emotion to touch whether he/she will feel comfortable or happy when they attempt to help every shoe customer to seek the most right shoe style in every shoe customer whole shoe searching processing. Othwerwise, serving robots are only one machine, they can not touch or feel every shoe customer individual emotion whether he/she feel comfortable or unhappy or happy when they need to contact them in whole shoe searching processing. Hence, I believe that some tasks robots can

not repalce human staff to do very easily. Otherwise, robots may bring disadvanatges to let any one businessman to loss his/her customers, due to robots can not touch every customer

emotion to compare human staff in service tasks more easily. Robots serving customer behaviors may cause money lose and customers number lose to the shop in micro economic view.

Intellectual human economic behaviors

What does intellectual human economic behaviors mean ? I believe that when we choose or decide to do intellectual behaviors, then our societies will be influenced to bring economic growth in consequence.I shall attempt to indicate pollution case to explain how and why eithet our intellectual or foolish behaviors may bring economic growth or recession in consequence as below:

On one hand, for air pollution social case aspect example, if we only consider to buy cars to drive for working aimr or holiday leisure aim. Then, our societies air will be polluted. Our health will be influenced to bad. Our car driving behaviors may cause global environment air pollution serously. In long tiem, global air pollution will bring our bodies health to be bad. Although, ourselves car driving behaviors may bring our driving travelling leisure enjoyment and comfortable feeling in short time, also we so not need to pay public transport fare often, but we need to compensate ourselves health economic intangible loss due to air pollution , when cars number increases, dirty air will cause ouselves health to become bad.

In the result, we will need to pay more medical expenditure when we are old age, due to ourselves bodies will become bad, due to we breathe global dirty air every day, due to ourselves cars pollute air in long time, e.g. 10 to 20 years, even 30 more without limited air pollution environment. So, driving cars behavior may be one kind of human foolish behavior and our foolish behavior may bring ourselves future long time medical expenditure absolutely.

One the other hand, water pollution social aspect, if we often keep much rubblish to pollute sea, oil exploration porcessing pollute ocean , ships gas pollute ocaen, then fishes will eat polluted food and drive dirty water, due to global ocean is polluted.

In fact, because human only to conside how to buy boats to carry on leisure enjoyment activities, or catch cruises to travel on the sea. Also, oil manufacturers only consider researching anywhere to find new oil exploration places to manufacture oil product, when their oil exploration processes pollute ocarn . Consequently, global fishes drink polluted warer or eat polluted food. They will have poison. SO, human will have high chance to eat poison polluted fishes, due to fishes are poison or are polluted.

So, human is doing foolish activities, we only hope to find oil exploration places to pollute ocean or we only spend money to buy ticket to catch ships to travel anywhere in global ocean. All of these human foolish behaviors will bring pollution to global ocean. On consequently, we will need to compensate to eat polluted or dirty or poision fishes, ourselves bodies health will be bad. In long time, we need have high chance to pay medical expenditure when we are old. So, pollution case may be one good example to explain how and why human foolish behavior may influence ourselves future need to compensate serious medical loss.

All of these human foolish behavior will bring pollution to global ocean. On consequently, we will need to compensate to eat polluted or dirty or poison fished , ourselves bodies health will be bad. In long time, we will have high chance to pay medical expenditure, when we are old. So, pollution case may be one good example to explain how and why human ourselves intellectual or foolish behaviors may influence future long time economic loss or economic growth or recession in micro and micro economic view.

On another water pollution aspect hand, if we often keep rubbish to sea, oil exploration processing pollutes ocean and ships' gas pollute ocean, then fishes will eat polluted food and drink dirty water, due to fishes will eat polluted food and drink dirty sea water because the global ocean is polluted seriously.

In fact, because human only consider how to buy boats to carry on any leisure water activities, or catches cruises to travel on the sea. Also, oil manufacturers only consider any where to find oil exploratin places to manufacture oil products from ocean, when their pol exploration processes can plooute ocean. Consequently, global fishes drink polluted water or eat direty food. They will have poison. So, human will have high chance to eat poison fishes.

Otherwise, such as pollutin case, it can infuence inflation or deflation. Consequently, the reason indicates supply and demand theory. If air pollution is serious, then we will consider health issue, global cars demand number may be influenced to reduce, when global cars number demand will reduce, global car prices and supply number will need to change to fall down in order to attract or persuade global car consumers choose to make car purchase decision.

Hence, global car manufacture number and car price will be influenced to reduce, due to global air pollution issue. Consequently, deflation will occur because when the country citizen usually does not spend much extra saving money to buy car expensive goods. Money value will be low. Otherwise, if global cair pollution is not serious, human considers to buy cars to enjoy driving leisure lives. So, global car demand is influenced to increase , also global car price will also influenced to increase.

Consequently, gobal human will choose to buy cars to drive. Due to we accept to spend extra saving to buy expensive car goods. Car sale price and supply may be influenced to rise up. Money value is influenced to reduce. Inflation may be influenced, due to global car consumers number increases, we would not have extra money to spend easily. Car expensive goods expenditure influences our spending habit to avoid to make car purchase decision more easily. So, human intellectual or foolish activities may bring inflation or deflation consequency in possible indirectly in macro economic view.

On conclusion, above pollution case explain that how and why human intellectual or foolish economic behaviors may bring inflation or deflation consequency as wll as economic growth or recession consequency as well as any goods demand and supply increasing or decreasing consequency. It implies that human behavior may have indirect relationship to influence any goods demand and supply number to either increase or decrease result as well as any goods price will be influenced to increase or decrease in micro and macro economic view.

The relationship between social change and human behavior

Why does economic changes may influence human individual behavioral change? I shall attempt to indicate shopping behavior and staying at home behavior to explain their case and effect relationsip as below:

Human behavior can be influenced by economic change or economic change can be influenced by human behavior? Why does recession may influence consumers reduce shopping desire? In social recession suitation, it is possible that many people lose jobs suddenly, due to businessmen lose many customers. They need to make decision to reduce employees number in order to continue to keep businesses. Consequently, many firms (organizations) their employees may lose jobs. When they have much time, due to lose jobs, they will feel to avoid to spend too much time and money to go to shopping often. Many losing jobs people, they will often stay at homes. So, they will reduce time to go to shopping, then non essential products won't their preferable choice purchase products. Hence, recession will change many losing jobs people their shopping or consumption desires to avoid to buy non essential products often . Usually when economic boom, many people have jobs to do because consumers number must increase when many people have jobs to do. Then, many people can accept to spend money to buy non essential products often. Many people feel spend time to go to shopping can satisfy their purchase of any kinds of new products useful psychology or desire. So, recession is one good example to explain it can influence many people do not like often to leave homes to go to shopping easily. Many people like to stay at homes, becaue they feel worry about spending too much shopping time when they leave homes. Their staying home time is one good negative shopping behavior example. So, economic change may influence human individual behavior changes , they have direct cause and efect relationship in behavioral economic view.

May human behavior influence economic change? Is it possible that human behavior may bring the country social economic change in macro economic or micro behavioral economic view ? I shall indicate publishing industry example. Do you feel that if there are many students feel learning is very important when they read many books or many of students feel interesting to read or they have reading new books in habit, then it is possible that the country will have many students like to spend time to go to any book shops to choose the books, they feel that they can help they learn new knowledge. Then the country will increase students number, they often spend time to visit any one book shop every week. Their visiting book shops behavior which may become their habits. So, the country will increase students number, they often spend time to visit book shops. Also, it implies that visiting book shops behaviors may be their behavioral habits.

So, when the country has many students often spend time to visit book shops , their visiting book shops behaviors may help any one book shop to raise books sale chance. So, the country's student individual often visiting book shop behaviors, their habitual visiting book shops behaviors must may assist help any one book shop to increase books sale number absolutely.

Consequently, any one book shop , its books sale bumber must be influenced to increase to increase because the country will have many students like or feel need visit book shops habit in order to choose any suitable books to buy to read at home in order to raise themselves learning effort. When the country has many bok shops often have many students visit their book shops, then their books sale number may be influenced to increase. It explain why student individual visiting book shop behavior may help any one book shop sale number increases also.

How human productive behavior may influence economic development

May any country which citizen behavior assist themselves country development? It is one cause and effect economic question. I mean that if the country itself citicen can not concentrate mind or energy to choose to do one kind of industry in order to let themselves country can bring the most benefit, then whether the counry itself economy can bring the most serious economic benefit. I shall attempt to indicate these countries themselves indistry choice to explain whether these countries themselves citizen productive behavior may help themselves countries to achieve the largest economic benefits. I shall indicate as below:

New Zealand farmer individual wine productive behavior

For New Zealand country example, this country concerns itself effort is foucs on farming agricultural aspect. So, this country has many farmers concentrate on farming agricultural aspect. May New Zealanders choose to spend time to produce different kinds of wines, e.g. wine or red grape wine is for the people are eating meat, or they are eating dinner.

When these New Zealanders their behaviors choose to do farming or agriculture to grow and produce different kinds of taste of white or red grape wine drinking products job. Themselves grape agriculture behavior will influence these New Zealanders themselves, they can learn how to improve different kinds of grape wine drinking products in order to achieve every kinds of white or read grape wines taste improving aim during their white or red grape producing process.

Why can New Zealander every individual white or read grape wine producers improve their white or read grape wine taste more easily? In behavioral economic view, it can explain that why any one New Zealander white or read grape wine producer can be encouraged or excited or persuaded to concentrate nervous and energy and effort to learn how to improve their white or red grape wine products easily.

In fact, New Zealand is one agricultural food export country. It has good natural environment resource , e.g. land, seed to provide any one farmer to produce themselves any kinds of agricultrual food products, e.g. fruit, or wine food products. Because New Zealanders know themselves country has enough natural resource . So, in common, many New Zealanders choose to attempt to do farming agricultural jobs in order to export themselves any kinds of fruit or meat or wine products to overseas or sell to domestic in order to earn profit.

So, when these New Zealand farmers number has been increasing every year. This country farmers will feel themsleves competition between this

New Zealand farmers themselves are serious due to they may feel New Zealanders choose to do agriculture businesses in order to export themselves different kinds of farming food to overseas or sell to local to earn profit.

Hence, when many New Zealand farmers feel that farmers number has been increasing every year. They will feel themselves competition is serious. They must need to spend much time and nervous and effort to research what method is the best how to produce the best taste of white or red grape wine products in order to let local or overseas wine buyers to choose to buy his/her producing white or read grpae products to drink.

Hence, in competition psychological view, may influence many New Zealand white or reaad wine producers had been beginning to change their learning behavior on researching what method is the best in order to produce the best quality of taste red or white wine products to sell in order to attract overseas or local white or read grape wine drinkers to choose to buy his/her wine products. Their behavior will focus on learning how to raising or improving white or read grape wine taste method more than only focus on producing a large number white or red grape wine products. They believe wine quality is more important to compare wine producing number. So, New Zealand wine producers themselves wine producers behaviors have been changing on concentrating on researching wine quality method aspect more then wine producing number aspect in behavioral economic view.

America high technological productive behavior

For America example, US is one high technological country, it owns many high technological knowledge talent inventors, e.g. computer science inventors. Hence, US must attract many diferent countries owning high technological computer inventors choose to go to US to develop their computer science profession career. Also, it seems that when many computer science inventors or professions choose to go to US to develop themselves computer science new career. In behavioral economic view, due to their leaving themselves countries choice, which may bring influence themselve country job behaviors need to be changed. They must need to adapt US new live. Because they will forgive their past computer science job. These computer science professionals need to spend time to adapt US new lives. They " past computer science job behaviors" will need to be changed to their new US any computer employer's new computer science job model.

Because their traditional computer science jobs needed to be forgot in their themselves countries. They will feel their old computer science job knowledge and behavior needed to change in order to let their US any one new of computer company employer feels satisfactory to accept their new working behavior in any one US computer organization.

So, on the other hand, many US computer company employer will feel that they must need time to accept any one new overseas computer science professions their working behaviors, their working attitude daily, because these foreign comouter science professional, their past computer working behaviors and working attitude must be different to US domestic computer science professions.

In behavioral economic view, these overseas computer science professions, their working behaviors and attitude must be needed to change in order to adapt any one US new computer company itself domestic or local computer science professional stafs themselves daily working behaviors and attitude because these overseas and local computer science professionals must need to team work together.

In behavioral economic view, it is only one way that foreign computer science professionals must need to change themselves past country traditiona daily working behaviors and attitude in order to cooperate with these US local computer science professionals in teams more easily.

Consequently, if these foreign compute science professionals can change their past working behaviors and attitude to let any one US local computer science professional feels to cooperate with them easily in short time. Then, the US computer company itself whole computer professional teams themselves efficiencies will be influenced to raised or improved by the changing past working attitude and working behaviors of these foreign computer science professionals. So, in behavioral economic view, only if US any one computer company hopes itself computer teams themselves efficiency can be raised or improved when it decides to employ foreign computer science professionals and US domestic computer science professionals. They need to work in teams together. They must need to let these foreign computer science professionals to know how to change their working behaviors and attitude to let their domestic computer science professionals feel easy to work together. Then, the US computer company itself whole team efficiency must be rasied or improved easily in short time.

● China share market investing behavior

For China share market example, economic development depends on financial market. Because if many Chinese have interest to invest to carry on shares buying and selling activities in orde to learn how to earn shares interest and share profit when the China shareholder can make decision to sell himself/herself shares in the the high price, then he/she can earn money when he/she can sell the China company's shares in the high sale share price position.

If China has many Chinese like to spend time to carry on investing shares activities. Themselves shares buying and selling behaviors will influence China has many companies can increase fund from many Chinese shareholders in order to have enough money to expand or develop themselves businesses in China in long term.

Consequently, when China can have many Chinese like to attempt to carry on buying and selling shares investing behaviors in China share market. Themselves buying and selling shares behaviors can help many Chinese companies have effort to increase enough money or capital in order to continue to do their businesses in long term absolutely. So, it explains why when many Chinese become sharcholders , they can assist China will have many companies continue to develop their businesses if many Chinese like to carry on shares buying and selling investing behaviors in long time in China financial investment market nowadays in behavioral economic view.

Why has any individual country have many people invest share behavior which can influence the country's macro consumption desire?

I shall apply shares market buying and selling investment behavior to explaiin why shares investment behavior which may impact the country's overal consumption desire as below:

In behavioral economic view, I assume that when the coutry has many people have interest to attempt to carry on shares buying and selling investment behavior, then their frequent shares buying and selling behaviors which may bring negactive consumption desire or shopping desire of these shares investors their consumer behavior.

The reason is simple, when the country has many share buyers number suddenly been increasing rapidly. Consequently, these large group share investors must need to spend much time to research any kinds of company shares variations, whether when their share prices will rise up of fall down in order to achieve buying the company's shares in the lowest price and selling the company's shares in the highest price level in order to earn profit. Basic on this reason, they must need to spend much extra time to research share prices changing behavior every day, e.g. one working person will wait to leave his/her job, after he/she can spend time to gather data to research the day's share price changing behavior after dinner. So, the working person's right time may be his/her share price market research behavior. Before he/she may spend his/her night time to go to shopping after dinner, but nowadays, he/she will fogive to do his/her shopping behavior before dinner or after dinner at hight sometime. He/she will make decision to spend much night time to turn on computer to click on share market website to research his/her share purchase choice to investigate whether his/her share price whether it rises up or falls down at the moment in order to make his/her share buying or selling decision at ever night time.

I mean the when the country has many people are share investors, their shares investment behavioral spenging time which will influence many shops lose customers at might often because the country will have many people feel need to spend night time to turn on computer or watch television to investigate share price variation. So, the country will have many people / share investors choose to stay at home in order to carry on share price variation investigation behavior, they need to listen share market update news from radios or watch the share market update news from computer or TV at home every night. Consequenly, they must reduce times to leave themselves homes at night. So, their shopping behavior also will be reduced. Because these share investors feel need to spend time to investigate share price variation news at homes which can bring economic benefits (high opportunity benefits) when they choose to forgive to leave homes to go to shopping times (opportunity cost) every night.

On conclusion, it seems that when the country has many people are share investors, then their share price investigating behavior may bring negative shopping emotion at night. Consequently, the country's any one shop may lose many customers from this share investor consumer group in behavioral economic view. Hence, when the country's share investors number had been increasing rapidly, it will influence any shops lose many customers from this share investing customer group at night frequenly in short time, even long time in behavioral economic view, because their shopping desires or shopping emotion will be brought negative feeling when they make decisions to spend much time to listen radios or watch TV or computers share price update nes at night. Hence, share market will bring negative impact to influence consumer shopping desire or negative shopping emotion in behavioral economic view.

Can technology influence human shopping behavioral change?
Nowadays, technological development has reached mature stage, whether

technological mature stage may bring positive or negative shopping emotion influence to global consumers. I shall aplly internet inventin or ecommerce shopping channel tool to explain whether internet technology can bring postive or negative influence to global consumer behavior in behavioral economic view.

Internet is a good technological tool, it brings e-commerce business chance. In fact, commonly, global has have many businessmen choose to use internet channel to carry on their products transactions between global online-buyers and their electronic websites. So, global many shoppers had begun to feel online shopping is more convenient to compare visiting shops shopping. Their shopping behaviors have been changed from internet technological tool. Global has many shoppers choose to buy any products from any overseas or local businessmen their web stores. They only need to spend time to find any businessmen their webstores to choose the most suitable products to pay visa to buy from their webstores. at homes. So, in general, global had have may shoppers had changed their shopping behaviors from visiting shops to visiting webstores at homes often.

So, it seems that internet technological tool had influenced global many shops disappear, but internet webstores will be replaced their actual shops on streets. Some of businessmen either they choose webstores to replace shops or choose websotes and shops both or still keep shops only. Hence, internet tool influences global businessmen have three kinds of products sale channels to let globa local and overseas consumers to choose how to buy their products.

However, in fact, many of global shoppers, youngers and olders had begun to accept to buy any products from webstores. They feel to spend time to leave homes to visit shops , their shopping behaviors will be wasted time to not essential part to their daily lives. Hence, since internet technological invention, it had changed many consumers their traditional visiting shops shopping habit to change to buying products from webstores channel.

However, on the one hand, internet creates webstores ecommerce shopping channel to let global many consumers do not need to leave homes to go to shopping. It brings negative visiting shops shopping emotion to global general consumers nowadays. But on the other hand, it also brings positive visiting internet webstores shopping emotion to global general consumer nowadays. So, it seems that global many consumers feel that they often do not need to spend much time to go out shopping. Many global consumers feel convenient and enjoy to choose any products to buy from different internet webstores, when the online buyer chooses the most suitable product, he she only needs to pay visa card to buy the product from the online seller's webstore conveniently at home.

Hence, online shopping can bring economic benefit to online buyers, e.g. avoiding walking time or spending transport fare to visit the shop to go to shopping, shortening or reducing shopping time to do another important matter.

On conclusion, global many consumers began feel online shopping can bring more economic benefits on shortening shopping time, avoiding transport fare spending aspect. So, online shopping will be popular shopping behavior for future long time. It may encourage global many shoppers can make rapid shopping decision in short time in order to carry on any products buying transaction to global any one online shopper in short time easily in behavioral economic view. So, global many businessmen had begun to build themselves one attraction webstore in order to persuade different countries consumers to choose to click themselves webstores from internet channel to buy any kinds of products in short time easily.

So, internet technology had changed consumers traditional shopping behaviors to build positive online shopping emotion as well as raise online sellers' any products sale chance easily in behavioral economic view.

Why and how human behavior may influence the country's economic growth or recession?

When one country has many people choose to do the same matter for one period, whether their behavior may influence the country's pvera; economic growth or recession . I shall attempt to indicate cases toexplain their relationship as below:

For flowing rubblish behavioral case example, do you feel that when the country has many people often flow rubblish on the streets, instead of their flowing rubblish behavior may bring streets dirty? But, their flowing rubblish behavior may explain that this country has people may have enough money to buy food to ear, or enough cloths to wear, enough bottles of water to drink, even they may have enough money to buy new television, radio, refrigeraters , washing machines, desktops or laptops electronic home products from old to new to use in order to satisfy their living needs. So, when they flow old electronic home products, their flowing old home electronic products behaviors may seem that they have enough money to buy other new home electronic products to replace old home electronic products to use at homes.

However, it seems thaat this country ought have many people have jobs to do. So, many of them, they can easy to make purchase decison to flow any old home electronic products and buy any new home electronic products to use . Because this country has many people have jobs to do. So, they can often not use old home electonic products to become rubblishs to flow on streets after they had bought any kinds of new home electronic homes.

In fact, it also implies that this country's economy grows rapidly. So, many businesses can glow up rapdly. When they expanded their businesses, they must need to increase employees number in order to let they help themselves to raise productivity or serve their clients absolutely. So, when the country has many businesses can grow up, it seems that its economy must be better or it is improved to compare past. Due to many different kinds of home electronic products had been often bought to use by this country people in this period. So, this country's any streets can be observed that expensive electronic home products were flowed on streets anywhere. then, this country will have many electronic home products sellers can sell their home electronic products very easily. When this country has many people can find any kinds of jobs to do easily. So, due to unemploymen rate had been decreasing.

In behavioral economic view, as this many electronic home products rubblish country case, we can observe this country may have many people have jobs to do. So, consumption number has been increased long time. So, cheap food, or expensive home electronic products may be rubblish on any streets. This country's people , their flowing rubblish behaviors may be explained that many of people have enough jobs to do, so they have ability to buy any good taste food to eat or buy any kinds of expensive electronic home products to use. So, this country's economy may be improved for this long period. So, in behavioral economic view, when this country can have many electronic home products rubblishs are flowed on anywherer in streets frequently. It seems that this country will have many people have jobs to do, so it causes they often change old home electronic products or replaced them easily, when they have enough income to spend to buy any kinds of new home electronic products to use at homes easily. Moreover, their flowing old electronic home products behaviors also indicate that this country has many people their salaries may be increased in possible from their emplyers. When this country can have many different kinds of home electornic products are sold. It means that this country's electronic home products needs or demand had been increasing, due to many people have jobs to do and income increases to excite their living of needs also improve. Consequently, this country may seem have better economic improvement. We can observe from this country's electronic home products rubblish increasing income in theis period.

On conclusion, this country ought experience economic growth at this period. So, " flowing expensive electronic home rubblish increasing number " may seem that this country's economic growth is rapidly in this period, due to many people have jobs to do as well as salaries increase in this period.

Technology how impacts human behavior changing?

Technology how influences human behavior to bring changing? For example, online share purchase and sale transaction from smart phone brings share investor can do share buying or selling transation in any where and any time conveniently, non manual driving auto vehicle, bring car owner feels comfortable and spends free time to do other matter, e.g. reading, listening mucis in himself or herself car freely. electrical energy vehicle can help car owner to reduce air polluton and it can brings the drivers do not feel drive long time in any journeys in order to avoid air pollution for environmental protection responsible car drivers in our societies. Thus, they will drive long time in any journeys when they can drive electronic energy cars to replace oil energy cars.

However, online technology can also bring consumers can choose to stay at homes to buy any things from seller individual online webstore conveniently. Such as online technology can bring shoppers do not need to spend much time to visit shops to buy any things. They can choose any kinds of products from any online sellers individual online webstores conveniently at homes. Online technology excite busy consumers can make purchase decision easily as well as it can help online sellers sell any kinds of products from internet easily.

In behavioral economic view, technology can change human behavior to be improved, it can let human feels comfortable, more free time ro use, rapid making any decisions, such as apply smart phones to make share purchase or sale transaction decision, online shopping decision, even travelling any where decision in short time, when the traveller finds the most cheap hotel accommodation room price and air ticket price frm any travel agent online tourism webstore, then the potential travel customer can follow the online hotel accommodation price and air ticket price data to make decision when to buy the air ticket from the airline travel agent or make decision when to prebook which hotel accommodation room to go to the country to travel from online travel agent tourism webstores. So, technology can encourage global any country travelers to make anywhere to trvel rapidly. If the traveler can find the country's general hotel rooms and airline tickets prices had been decreasing more sightly. The traveler may make travel decision to choose the country to travel in short time, then he/she can prebook the country;s any hotel room and airline ticket to pay by visa fraom the country's any hotel and airline travel agent webstores., before one week, even one month or more easily. Hence, online technology can also encourage traveler individual frequent travel times to be increased, due to global travelers can find any hotel rooms and airline tickets prices from internet conveniently at homes. They do not need to spend time to visit any airline travel agent to enquire travel choice country's hotel rooms prices and airline ticket prices. They can compare global travel of countries choices ' all hotels rooms and airline agents air tickets prices to make prebook airline seat and hotel room decision before one week, one month even six months early.

On conclusion, online technology can encourage global travelers can make travelling any where and when traveling time desicions easily. It can excite tourism industry develops in long time. Also, such as electricity cars invention can encourage environment protection car owners do car purchase decision easily, because they can choose to drive electronic energy cars to replace oil energy cars in order to avoid air pollution occurs easily. So, electronic cars can increase electronic car purchasrs number, due to many of environmental protection attitude of car owners can choose to drive electricity cars to bring air cleans, even non -manual driving cars can encourage lazy driving and free time driving car owners to choose to buy non-manual (artificial intelligent) cars to drive , because they can spend much free time to read, listen music or do any matters in themselves cars, they do not need to drive cars, robotic (AI) auto driving machine is such one non-manual driver to help them to drive themselves cars confidently. So, non-manual driving cars can attract lazy and enjoying free time driving car owners to choose to buy to replace traditional manual cars to drive easily. Moreover, online share transaction can help any share investors to make share buying and selling decision in short time easily. When they can apply smart phones technological tool to carry on share buying and selling activities easily. They can observe any share rising or falling price suitation from smart phones in any where any any time easily. So, smart phone technology can help global any shareholders to make share purchase and sale transaction easily. So, technology can encourage human makes decision in short time rapidly.

How and why employees behaviors may influence economy development?

In behavioral economy view,I believe the country's any organizational employees behavior may bring indirect relationship to influence the country's long term economic development. I shall indicate past manufacture industry social development period to explain their relationship. For many countries' past business activities had belonged to manufacturing industry, such as US, UK past before 1980 year, it focused on steel manufacturing and steel manufacturing related machine products. So, US, Uk developed countries manufacturing industries may be past main country's economic income sources. I assume US , UK past had one million number different kinds of industries. They ought had about seven houndred thousand number organizational businesses were belonged to manufactured industry. They may include:

Steel manufacturing and steel related machine manufacturing, e.g. vehicle manufacturing, home appliances, e.g. washing machine, television, radio, refrigerate cooler, heater, air condition etc. different kinds of different kinds of steel -related manufacturing machine, they were manufactured from US, UK steel machine manufacturers. So, US, Uk the other three hundred thousand number industry may be general service industry, e.g. hotel service, restaurent, cinema, public transport service, tourism lesiure , wine bar, supermarket etc. different kinds of non-manufacturing industries business organizations were operated in UK, US past before 1980 year.

So, in UK, US developed countries industry development history, they ought have high percentage of businesses belonged to steel related manufacturing machine and steel products. Also, in the past before 1980 year, US, Uk business employers , they employed many workers are manufacturing workers. They needed to spend long time to work in factories. They were skillful workers, and they are trained to manufacturing cars, washing machine, television, heater, etc. even steel itself different kinds of steel related products to prepare to deliver to their shops to sell to US, Uk local or overseas clients.

So, I believe that past UK, US ought employ many employees, they belonged to skillful manufacturing workers, manufacture increasing steel machine or steel related machine number of products rapidly daily. So, if UK, US had

had many of these manufacturing factories owned high skillful workers, then their manufacturing steel-related machine or steel both kinds of products number must be influenced to raise rapidly. Consequently, their steel machine manufacturing products would been exported to overseas or would been sold to local both markets , they may be influenced to raise sale number. They (these manufacturing workers) needed to be trained to know how to manufactur these different kinds of machine products in the efficient teams and they ought to be trained to raise their efficiencies in order to shorten time to manufacturing many kinds of steel related manufacturing machine or steel itself products rapidly. So , if their efficiencies and manufacturing performance was improved, these US, UK any one manufacturing worker and their teams ought achieve raising productivities significantly.

Hence, when past UK, US manufacturing industry development period, if these two countries' any manufacturing factories could have many manufacturing workers could be trained to be skillful and proficient manufacturing workers. Then, in past every day to these factories workers, they ought help their steel or steel related manufacturing employers to raise any kinds of machine or steel products number in every team. So, when past in the manufacturing industry development, US, UK could have many factories' manufacturing workers themselves steel or steel related machine products manufacturing skill could be trained to to improve to any kinds of these machine or steel manufacuring products quality as well as their products number could be influenced to raise by themselves skillful improvement significantly every day.

Then, what would be influenced to occur to past UK, US manufacturing industry period? In behavioral economic view, when these two manufacturing industry developed countries, such as UK, US , if they had many factories workers can be trained to improve their skill in order to achieve any kinds of steel or steel-related machine products quality could be improved as well as products manufacturing number could be also increased absolutely.

In consequence, past UK and US both countries ought increase themselves any kinds of steel and steel related machine products number to be supplied to themselves local shops to let local clients to choose any one kind of machine manufacturing products to buy easily as well as they could also export to supply overseas any countries to buy their different kinds of steel or steel related machine products to let overseas steel or steel related manufacturing machine product buyers, they can have many of these different kinds of these steel or steel-related different kinds of manufacturing machine from UK and UK these both countries easily to compare other countries.

On conclusion, I believe that past US, and UK macro manufacturing industry income GDP would increase significantly. So, they would have good economic growth performance because when many of these manufacturing workers themselves manufacturing effort could be improved. So, it explained when employees manufacturing abilities can influence economic growth indirectly.

Robots invention whether they can help organizations to raise efficiencies or inefficiencies?

In behavioral economic view, in any organizations, when the organization hopes its worker teams can raise efficiencies , the organization may choose to increase more workers number and/or it can provide training to improve these workets themselves skills in order to raise their efficiencies. For one warehouse example, when the warehouse increases many goods , they are needed to delivered these goods from the shelves to the delivering destination locations. If this warehouse supervisors feel these workers themselves goods delivery speeds are slow, which is possible due to this warehouse's workers number is not enough. So, this warehouse supervisor ought increase workers number in order to increase their goods delivery speed in order to deliver goods from the shelves to every indicated goods delivery destination in order to let any one lorry driver can transport the right kinds of goods and ensure the accurate goods number to transport to any one client home rapidly.

However, if this warehouse supervisor planed to buy several warehouse goods delivery robots to assist these warehouse workers to find the right kinds of goods from shelves and then deliver to the right destination location in the warehouse. So, these warehouse orkers can concentrate on counting the accurate goods number and ensuring the right kinds of goods in order to prepare to let lorry drivers to transport these goods to these goods of buyers themselvers homes rapidly. Consequently, in the first step, robots can concentrate on finding th right goods from shelves and delivers them to the right goods transportation of location destination. Then, in the second step, these warehouse workers can concentrate on counting the accurate goods number and ensuring the right kinds of goods in order to prepare to put them to the lorry. Consequently, when warehouse robots and warehouse workers can cooperate to work together, the most important, robots, can deal on finding the right kinds of goods and deal on delivering the accurate number of goods of job duty as well as these warehouse workers can only concentrte on counting the right kinds of goods number in order to avoid it has none any mistake of wrong kinds of goods and inaccurate goods of delivery number to be transported to the lorry and to deliver to any one buyer's home.

So, it seems that warehouse robots ought help any one warehouse worker to raise himself efficiency and avoid goods delivery of mistake occurrence easily as well as their help to warehouse workers that can let any one goods buyer feels their goods can be delivered to their homes rapidly. Moreover, warehouse robots can also help these warehouse workers to raise efficiencies because warehouse robots can help them to shorten goods delivery time between any one shelf and any one goods delivery destination of location in the warehuse because robots may help them to find the right kinds of goods from the right shelf in the short time. So, any one worker does not need to spend long time to seek anywhere is the right shelf location for the kind of goods when the kind of goods are needed to deliver to the buyer's home from lorry. Warehouse robots can help them to do this aspect of " finding the goods from the right shelf in short time job duty". So, any one warehouse worker only needed tospend less time to do the counting of any right kind of goods number and ensuring the right kind of goods job duty. Consequently, this warehouse 's any one worker, his any one kind of goods delivery time may be reduced, because robots' assistance and they may have more confidence to avoid mistake to deliver the wrong number of goods and/or the wrong kind of goods to any one goods buyer's home.

On conclusion, it seems that warehouse robots ought may help any one warehouse worker to raise efficiency for any one team in the warehouse as well as the warehouse any one supervisor does not need to spend much time to observe any one worker individual performance for " goods delivery job duty aspect" because their goods delivery job duty that had been replaced to do by these several warehouse robots. Robots can achieve the more accurate of right kinds of goods and the right number of goods delviery job performance to compare any one of human warehouse worker themselves right kinds of goods of delivery and right number of goods of delivery job performance. So, when robots can participate to cooperate with this warehouse's any one worker to do their goods of delivery job duty in this warehouse every day. Then, robots can raies any one of supervisor individual confidence in order to let they do not need to spend time to observe any one of worker individual whose goods of delivery job performane. They can concentrate on supervising any one worker whose goods transport to lorry in the final step in order to avoid to deliver wrong goods number and / or wrong kind of goods to any one goods buyer's home every day. Consequently, this warehouse's overall teams of their delviery of goods performance many be improved by robotss' participatin to goods of delivery task as well as this warehouse's oveall teams themselves efficiencies may be influenced to raise by robots' goods of delivery task participation.

Why social behavior may influence organizational strategy needs to be changed ?

Why any organizations need to know whether nowadays social behaivor how has been changing in order to implement the kind of the most right strategy to achieve the profit aim pursue in possible. I shall indicate nowadays ecommerce or online, customer shopping behavior to explain above question concerns they ought have close relationship between social behavior and organizational strategic choice or organizational behavioral changing need.

On nowadays ecommerce business, or online shopping model, this kind of shopping model in global many young and old age consumers like to apply internet tool to choose any country sellers website stores in order to stay at home to buy any kinds of products from themselves webstores in global societies.

In fact, online shopping model had been popular for long time above to twenty years. Most of global sellers will make decision to design themselves webstores in order to attract global many online buyers to choose to buy their products from themselves webstores. So, it seems that social consumers purchase behaviors had been changed to online shopping from internet invention.

Hence, social consumers purchase behavioral changes may influence any organizations' strategies need to be changed from visiting shops purchase strategy model to online purchase strategy model, if the seller still concentrate on concentrate on considerate how to design itelf , but neglects to considerate how to design itself webstore, e.g. how to design attract product photos to put on itself webstore, how to arrange sale price information location to be putted on webstore and visa card payment location on itself webstore in order to let any one online buyer can feel very easier to buy itself any kinds of products from itself webstore. Then, its potential online buyers will be influenced to increase number when they can find this online seller itself any kinds of products photes and every kinds of product sale price information and visa card payment channel locations easily from itself webstore.

So, it implies that nowadays any one seller ought need to design one webstore to let any one online overseas and domestic consumers can have chance to click itself webstore to choose any one kind of product to buy conveniently when he/she does not hope to leave him/her home to go to shop, because nowadays social shopping behaviors had been influenced to change when internet invention, them it gives another online purchase method to replace visiting shops purchase method to global any one buyer in nowadays societies.

So, if nowadays any one seller still concentrate on how to design itself shop display in order to put any kinds of product on shelf in order to let any one visiting shop customer to find the kind of product to buy, but it neglects to change to choose to pursue another new technological shopping method, such as webstore purchase method in order to implement effective strategy to design the most right webstore as well as in order to attract global overseas and local consumers to find itself webstore easily from website and find its any one kind of product phots and sale price and visa card payment button in order to choose to buy itself any kinds of products in the short time. Consequently I believe that the seller will lose many customers from overseas and local when its other same or similar product sellers choose to design themselves webstores in order to let global any one product buyer can buy themselves any one kind of product when they can pay visa card to buy their products from them webstores conveniently when they stay at home habitly. Then, the seller will lose many global potential customers in long time.

On conclusion, in behavioral economic view, any consumer behavioral social changing, which will influence any in order to avoid customers number loses significantly . In future time, organizations need to make rapid decision in order to implement the most reasonable and the most useful strategy in order to avoid global potential customers number reduces or lose them in long time. So, social behavioral changing environment ought influence any global organizations need to decide how to change themselves strategies in order to avoid customers loses significantly in future time.

FIVE

WHAT ARE ORGANIZATIONAL HARD AND SOFT SKILLS

● Skills shortages on developing country market

Future developing countries need to develop their economy, so they need to employ many employees who own technical skills and /or soft skills. What kind of technical skills and/or soft skills , the developing countries' employees who will need to order to raise competiton in local job market ? I shall indicate the developing country China example. China is one developing country, employers will need different kinds of skillful labors to assist them to develop their businesses. However, China employers will face skillful labour shortage challenge. Although Chinese young age population is high, but many of them do not to be encouraged to learn enough skillful knowledge to fill future new skillful positions. So, the fast speed of training will be important to influence China supply and demand labour market to be more accurately as well as future China's the quality of labour demand number will be influenced to be raised after they have enough training to learn new skills.

How to solve future China skillful shortage of labour? Firstly, nowadays, China employers need to teach their employees to learn how to use and how to operate robotic skills in China's factories. AI robotic has been early developing, so they need to prepare to learn robotic management and operating technical and soft skills in order to satisfy future China factory automation industry development.

China is one world's factory for low-end products to high quality information products, high end technology and services. So, China will need many high skilled workers to assist manufacturers to manufacture many different kinds of products to export or local sale. Moreover, robotic manufacturing skillful workers will also need because robotic will be accepted to assist manual workers to work in China's any factories. This has led to greater demand for labour wirh upgraded skills and competence. So, it seems that China's orkers need to lern any high technological manufacturing knowledge, e.g. learning how to co-operate with robotics to raise productive efficiencies, which will be future many China's manufacturers' skills need intention.

So, when any one of China manufacturer invests robotics to work in its factory . Then, the China manufacturer's labours ought need to know how to co-operate with th robotics to raise productivities and efficiencies. Moreover, these China service industries, e.g. IT, software, accounting, finance, marketing and customer service management, e.g. waiter, property security, shopping center customer service etc. service occupations. In the future, robotics can also used to participate any one of these service industries' part of tasks in order to raise service performance. So, any one of these service industries' employees need to learn how to operate with robotics in order to achieve the most excellent servvice performances to satisfy consumers' needs. So, China service industries labours ought need to learn how to co-operate or manage service natural robotics to work together more efficiently because future China manufacturers will prefer to employ the labours who know how to co-operate and manage and control any service natural robotics more easily and efficiently in order to achieve the most excellent service performance to satisfy customers needs.

Hence, it seems that China manufacturing and service workers need to spend time and effort to learn how to co-operate with manufacturing natural robotics to manufacture any products in factories efficiently or deliver any cargos in warehouses more efficiently or serve customers to let them to feel excellent service performance in restaurants or shopping centers or properties or offices receptions counters. Then, when their China employers apply robotics to participate to work in factories, restaurants, shopping centers, cinemas, offices or properties reception etc. different working places . These low skillful labours will be dismissed easily, due to robotics can replace them to manufacture any products or provide services to satisfy clients' needs in order to let them to fell robotics' performances are more excellent to compare human service labours or their productive efficiencies are more effort to compare workers. So, future China workers need to learn how to cooperate or manage or contol with robotics to work more efficiently, if they do not expect to be dismissed easily.

● Future global skillful labor soft knowledge skill need

In the future several occupations have been identified as the most frequent movers between all labour market states. The elementary occupations include: waiters, bar staffs, clearners, catering assistants, construction and security service workers, care workers, sales assistants and general clerks etc. So, the low educational level workers can learn these soft wkills to raise whose professional workering level to prepare to do these above positions in global elementary occupation job market.

The changes of employer were most frequent for IT programmers, doctors, electricians, carpenters, skilled workers in global labour market. These skilled occupations will have manpower shortage supply challenge, due to either people feel the educatonal level is under low. So, there has no many people have interest to know these knowledg to prepare their elementary careers. So, these kinds of low skilled occupations will have not enough human power supply to global labour job market also, the high skilled or educational job support.

Moreover, the high skilled occupations also encounter labour shortage issue. The skills in short supply related to experienced canadidates e.g. five years or more. For example, pharmaceutical , biogharma and food innovation industries. The occupational shortage roles include: Chemists, analytical scientists, product formulation, analytical development for roles in biopharma, quality control analyst includes pharmaco-vigilance, i.e. drug safety roles. The demand for engineering industry aspect which will aos increase the labour shortage includes process and design (research and development, quality control, automation, lean processes) are skillful labours need to help employers to achieve these intentions. They may include raising competitiveness, boosting productivity and skills availability. So, if future these above any one of occupation labours can not achieve these benefits to satisfy their employers' needs. Then, his/her average weekly or hourly wages will be reduced. It means that the unskilled labour under skilled labour wage can not increased more easily, even they own many year working experiences in any one of above these occupations. If the employer feels the labour is unskilled or below skilled level for any one of these occupations in these any one industry aspect, e.g. wholesale and retal , human health, education, accomodaton and food , construction, professional activities, financial service , public administration, and defence, transportation etc. occupations. Then, these industries' unskilled or below skilled level workers' salaries will be lower level to compare the higher skilled workers who work in any one of these industries.

The reason why future employers need to employ skilled labours. One explanation for slow recovery in demand in negative impact on investment is a prolonged period of high unemployment. This is led to job weekers left labour market or became unemployable due. So, future low skillful level will be one important factor to cause unemployment in society as well as nowadays labours ought need consider whether their skills are needed to improve in order to avoid future competition in job market.

2.1 Why do future labours need to learn worldwide readiness skills

Future employers need employees own worldwide readiness skills, such as reading , writing and arithmatic. Why do employees need worldwide readiness skills? In the future, high economic growth countries need high wage positions, high opportunity jobs which need a large number of skills required of job candidates of these positions " job readinss" and not " job training" , which support developments of these importance and widely desired skills won't only support the success to high-opportunity positions, but also be developed for future success in the competitive global economy. Because real-time business intelligence is needed for the talent marketplace to employ talent employees. So, it explains that it will have many future employers hope to employ owning readiness skillful employees to help them to develop their businesse intelligently. Hence, present employees ought need to hard to train readiness skills to prepare whose future employers' job requirements in the future competitive global job market.

2.2 Why these occupations need readiness skills

In the future these occupations will need to raise readiness skills. For example, mathematical science, teachers (post-secondary), management analysts, computer and information systems, managers, first-line supervisors of construction traders, solar photovoltaic installers. All of these occupations , employers need staffs to own good readiness analytic ability to help them to do more accurate real-time business intelligent decisions. The representative occupations include oral and written communication skills, project management, teamwork, marketing and creativity . Moreover, they need to own specific technology skill, deep science and math or even most business skills as well as these skills are "soft" skills more than hard skills. These kinds of occupation employees need own cooperative effort, creativity, problem solving, detail orientation and integrity personal characteristics, which are relevant across all knowledge and domains.

Therefore, in the future, science, technology,engineering and mathematics relevant occupations need to own more readniness and analytic skills more than othe kinds of occupations. Because these organizations need those professionals on knowledge acquisition, literacy analysis, synthesis and critical thinking skills that will impact their organizations to bring more critical thinking beneficial team culture. These occupational top skills will include oral and written communication skills, project management skill, team oriented skill, marketing and creativity skills, problem solving skill, detail oriented skill, self-motivated skills, management and analytical skills, coaching skill, business process modeling skills, work independent skill, strong leadership skills, management experience and business requirements gathering. All of these skills which will be future employers who need to employ these kinds employees who own these skills in preference. Also, all of these skills concentrate on soft skills more than hard skills. It seems that when above occupational applicants who own any one of thes skills, evn more than one skills. Then, he/she will have more chance to be selected to employ. Also occupation specific skills requirements are more needed to compare cross-functional skills for above of any one occupation. Because the high concentraton of cross-functional skills require " job readiness" and not " job training" for success, e.g. communicaton, integraton and presentation skills, entrepreneurialism and related skills, microsoft office software skills.

Of particular interest is communication, integration and presentation skills. These skills include ability to seek, evaluate and examine information and data create a reasoned position, present findings and make a case for or advocate for position. So, these skills are very important and they can help future applicants who expect to win any kinds of these positions easily. However, the hard skills can help these applicants to be more successful to win any kinds of these positions when they own these hard skills, e.g. microsoft offic, powerpoint, excel , word, microsoft project etc. softwares.

In conclusion, the global economy is dynamic and many of the skills required for positons in the future will need good technologies and work practices to be developed. The number of skills required t be successful in the jobs forecast to be most in demand in the future is growing. So, it explains that why future any one of these occupations which will need soft skills more than hard skills, due to organizations like to employ the employees who own managerial and analytical effort more than hard skills productive effort to assist their organizations to develop more easily.

2.3 Data -analysis skill needs

In the future, most organizations will have a number of jobs that include data analysis. Economists and labor market forecasters predict occupations need data analytical skill will need much. In addition, fast technological development means th types of technologies and applications workers in this field will need to be familiar with data analytical skill rapidly. It seems that data analytical jobs will have new job opportunity to employees with in-demand skills in future global labor market.

Why and how do employers demand for data analysis skills? Data analysis skills mean the ability to gather, analyze and draw practical conclusions from data as well as communicate data findings to others. The occupations include: data analyst, data scientist, statistician, market research analyst, financial analyst,research manager. In business career, many employers expect to employ statisticans, operations researh analysts, market research analysts and marketing specialists to assist their organizations to gather useful data from market in order to analyze and draw practical conclusions and finding the best solutions or methods to win their competitors.

Therefore, these data analysis jobs will have much need. Large size organizations with 500 or more employees were more likely than small or medium size organizations with 25 to 499 employees to plan hired data analysis positons in the future. For example, human source department will use big data to help make strategic decisions. How HR uses big data . HR will use big data for sourcing, recruitment, or selection, identifying causes of turnover and/or employee retention strategies or trends, managing talent and performance. Why organizations do not use big data. It is possible that they lack of knowledg expertise, the majority of organizatons will have data analysis positions within accounting and finance department, human resources department, business and administration department, information technology department, marketing, advertising and sales department, supply chain and operations department, research and development department, customer service department and other departments. So, future data analysis skill will need to used in different organizational departments.

However, publicly and privately owned for-profit organizations were more likely than government organizations to have data analysis positions in the marketing, advertising and sales function. Also, data analysis skills are required to different levels in any organizations , such as entry level, non-management / individual contributor level, mid-level management level, seniot management or executive level. The analyst, research analyst, market research analyst, scientist-based titles include: data scientists , research scientist, scientist, other descriptive titles include researcher, statistician, mathematician and other . So, data analysis positions will have many different skills to be selected to any one data analysis professional. For example, the data analysis professional can select either to learn the ability to interpret and communicate data analysis results skill or to learn how gathering or analyzing data skill. So, data analysis skill is not onlyone skill, it is more than one skill to let any one employee to select to learn.

Why do organizations need data analysis professionals? On workforce planning aspect, organizatons expect to let strategic direction and content of workforce needed for future business objectives easier, analyzing workforce: supply analysis, demand analsis and gap analysis more earier, developing action plan : recruiting and training plans to deal with gaps more easier, implementing action plan, monitoring, evaluating and revising plan more easier. So, organizations expect the data analysis professionsla can help them to solve these challenges, such as using of advanced technology solutons to integrate disparate planning sources; data availability and format; accessing to and understanding of the organization's data and analytics, developing business case to gain support from senior management and collaboration among HR staff, managers and executive easier. Future industries need data analysis professionals may include manufacturing health care and social assistance, scientific and technical service, finance and insurance, educational services , government agencies, retail trade, transportation and warehousing, construction, utilities, accomodation, and food services, waste management and remediation services, entetainment, and creation, real estate and rental and leasing , repair and maintenance, agriculture, forestry, fishing and hunting, personal and laundry services etc.

In conclusion, data analysis job need explains why future readiness and data analytical skills will be popular needed in globl labour market , due to these both skills are labour shortage and employers will need employees own big data readiness and data analytical both skills in order to win whose competitors more easier.

2.4 What are regional dynamic skills
of global labour market demand

Businessmen expect to improve better economic environment, they will prefer to recruit the most sought after skills of intelligent employees to bring positive beneficial impact to organizations. However, technology and digisation has had a significant influence on workers. Future globalization will trend digital economic development. Hence, it will influence workers' skills to be changed also. In fact, not all changes are positive because some workers will possible lose jobs, either due to new technology replaces their jobs or they lack enough effort to improve their skills in global digital economic labour market environment.

It brings this question: What are regional dynamic skills need whn digital busines environment is growing. In fact, organizations will continue to deal with skills shortages, labour markets across the global are continually changing. so, more employers and workers will need to adopt innovate working pattern, e.g. on call jobs, freelance jobs will grow popularly. The greater flexibility afforded to employ regardly.

Finally, digitalisation includes artificial intelligence, big data , online platforms. All these new technology will influence future employees how to worker. For example, they can apply online platform to work at home conveniently. So, they do not need to go to offices. They can finish their jobs and send to their employers by email easily. This kinds of job pattern can raise efficiencies and employers do not need go to offices often.

An important implication of innovating working which needs the employees who own digital skills in order to serve organizations more efficiently. So, employers are increasingly able to access demographics that were hitherto less active in labour markets. For example, future more women are joining the labour market because part time and self employment opportunities make it easier. This kinds of job pattern can raise efficiencies and employees do not need go to offices often.

An important implication of innovating working which needs the employees who own digital skills in order to serve organizations more efficiently. So, employers are increasingly able to access demographic that were hitherto less active in labour markets. For example, future more women are joining the labour market because part time and self employment opportunities make it easier to manage family with work life. So, digital skilling needs will cause many women lose jobs in possible. If the women lack digital job skills. Because high digital skill occupations need, like those requiring research, medical treatment and architectural design occupational digital skills are more common in the services sector, more women who own digital skill who can compete to win.

High digital skill occupations more easier than men because employers usually select female to do high skill occupations easier than make. However, if those professional service female employees can not learn how to apply digital skills to do these researchs medical treatmentm architectural design professional service jobs. Then, it is also different for these professional service femal employees to raise competition in global labour professional service market. So, these professional service female employees need to learn how to apply digital to do themselves jobs in future global professional service labour market. Otherwise, if the male professional service employees can attempt to learn how to apply digital skill to do themselves jobs in order to improve efficiencies and service performance to satisfy patients, such as medical service needs, school search service needs, construction firms' building needs. Then, the owning high digital technology skillful female employees will be more easier to find the professional service jobs which need digital skill more easier than the lacking digital skill female service professionals in future global digital service professional labour market.

On the other robotic communication skill need aspect, future employers expect workers to know how to communicate with robots to work efficiently in any working environment if the employers need robotc to serve their organizations. For example, communication between the robots on factory floors, and between people and robots could allow robots to start and stopr processes based on real-time conditions around them and alert people when there is a problem, so robots could increase their own efficiency if the workers could monitor themselves and determine when they needed maintenance; efficiency would also be improved if machines and robots could make production decisions on their own by. For example, ordering new suppliers when existing inputs into a production process run low. The increase in productivity of industrial robots will likely reduce the number of manual jobs on the shop floor.

At the same time, the increased output made possible by such robots will mean that manufacturers need more people in accounting, finance, sales, advertising and other roles. The increase in putput may also drive increased employment on manufacturers' supply chains. Hence, future employers expect to employ the workers who can know how to communicate with robots to work efficiently in order to raise productivity in any working environment. It means that it the worker can know how to control and communicate with the robots to work together in the team. Then, his/her communication and controlling robotic skill will help the organization's team to work efficiently and raise productivity in order to reduce time waste and human waste and resource waste considerately. So, future shortage of communication and controlling robotic skillful workers number will increase. It has much beneficial to workers who choose to attempt to learn how to communicate and control robots to work together in any working environment team efficiently. Because future employers will like to use robots to assist manual workers to attempt to raise productive efficiency in any working environment. So, the need of employees who know how to cooperate or communicate with robots whose talent skills will be useful to any future employers.

Future global business leaders will need human machine cooperation skill. This technological skill includes artificial intelligence (AI and internet of things (IOT), will reshape our working change. These machines will participate to our daily working environment. For instance, many business leaders agree that automated systems will free-up their time as well as they also believe they'll have more job satisfaction by offloading the tasks that they don't want to do to intelligent machines.

Therefore, future leaders will expect humans and machines can work as integrated teams within their organizaton in order to their workforce and machines are already successfully working this way. So, they need to expect future employees can know or learn how to work with automated systems more easily, because many jobs will be participated by automated systems, e..g simple accounting tasks, legal administration tasks etc. clerical tasks. They will be participated with (AI) technology, it learns how to cooperate with (AI) technology to finish simplt clerical tasks efficiently.

Future workers will need have autrmated system operational skills: They include that how to operate automated systems to free -up workers' time. Workers will need to learn how to operate automated system to better with healthcare tracking devices workers will need to learn how to operate automated systems to absord and manage information in completely different ways. Workers will need to learn how to operate automated systems of smart machines to work as admin. in any orking environments. Workers need be needed to learn how to operate (AI) automated machines to mak more accurate clerical tasks or efficiencies. So, the automated system (robotic) operational skillful workers' demand and number will increase.

In the future, employers need automated machine manufacturing and service with workers cooperation reasons include that clear protocols, will need to be established if autonomous machines fail. So, they need their workers to learn how to control and manage and communicate with autonomous machines skillfully. They believe move they depend upon technology, the more they'll have to lose in the event of a cyber attack. So, skillful workers are real required to let them to know how to cooperate with autonomous machines more efficiently and easily. Computers will need to be able to decipher between good and bad commands, so future employers have much chance to need the owning automated machines operating workers to assist any robots to make more accurate good or bad decision when robots and workers have need to make immediate judgement in their any related job responsibilites aspect.

Therefore, future owning automated machines operating workers' skillful level will be high. It bases on automated machine manufacturing environment trend factor. Finally, future technology will connect the right employee to the high task at the right time. It implies that when future global employers began to accept to apply robots to help them to raise any productivities efficiently. It will influence many manufacturing positions which need to employ any proficient skillful workers who own automated machines operational skills to know how to communicate or manage or control , even supervise any robots to work in teams in any organizational manufacturing environment efficiently.

In the future, employers also expect employees to own sufficient digital vision and strategic skills, manifest among other things. They can know how to apply data to demonstrate any senior support and sponsorship digital technological skill. They expect to reduce a skill gap and avoid a lack of employee buying and a workforce culture to change in their digital technologicl manufacturing organizations. Future employers also believe outdated technology that can't work fast enough, data overload, privary and security concerns. So, it explains why it is possible that future employers also need digital working environment and automated robots machines to attempt to achieve raising productive efficient aim.

Moreover, it also explains why digital transformation need will be raised. The reasons include: They feel digital technology can gain employees' buying in , making customer experience a boardroom concern, achieving fair compensation , training and goals and strategy achievement more easily, tasking senior leaders with digital working environment change putting policies and technology to support a fully remote, flexible workforce , empowering lines of team work more efficient, teaching all employees how to code/understanding how to adopt to work with automatic machines or rots in any team efficiently. So, automate machine can raise efficiency in manufacturing society.

In conclusion, in the future business society, employees need to be stronger human machine partnerships. So , future manufacturing or service industries will have digital technology and automated machine robotic technology to assist workers to work in any working environment efficiently. They expect digital technology and automated machine robotic technology anticipation to workers' daily jobs in order to bring positive impacting to the customer experience from business owners to decision makers in marketing, customer service, research and developmnt and finance etc. They also expect technological productivity can bring positive relationship between technology and workers emerging technologies' impact on business and the way workers and automated machine work together.

● Future organizational skill needs how to influence workforce
change to what kinds of employees

In the future whether in general organizations need what kinds of employees' skills, they expect employee individual own. It is one interesting question. The common skills that employees need to own in order to any duties to any organizational departments efficiently, e.g. human resource, marketing, administrative, logistic etc. different departments. For hospital, school, business, professional occupations etc. different organizations. Whether future school ought implement one system educational method to teach different common skills to students in order to let them to leave schools to jobs more easier.

Future employers need to create new technologies including automation and algorithms, in order to create new high quality jobs and improve the job quality and productivity of the existing work of human employees in any organizations, e.g. accounting department will need intelligence (AI) to assist account clerks to do simple repeating accounting job tasks in order to share their work load and raise performance efficiency or legal organizations will need (AI) to assist law clerks to do simple repeating legal draft or legal document revising job tasks . All future general clerical jobs will apply (AI) technological tools to assist human to job, it will produce a comprehensive platform for managing workforce change.

Hence, human manual(employees) need to learn how to adopt (AI) job participation to assist them to do different kinds of simple clerical jobs in any organizational administrative departments . They , clerical employees or white color workers need to learn how manage or dominate (AI) tool to improve job performance to be better. However, (AI) administrative workforce change, it is not only one kind of job automation change role in any physical offices. It influences future administrative clerks need change a more flexible manner, utilizing remote staffing beyond physical offices and decentralization of operations organizational workforce change.

Instead of (AI) participation to administrative job aspect, (AI) will also participate to manufacturing industry environment aspect, a new human-machine manufacturing workforce change will exist to any factories, warehouses working environment. Scientists predict that in present an average of 71% of total task hours across the industries are performed by humans, compared a 29% by machines. In this average is expected to have shifted to 58% task hours performed by humans and 42% by machines. In fact, nowadays, in terms of total working hours, no work task was yet estimated to be predominantly performed by a machine or an algorithm (AI). But, this picture is predicted to have somewhat changed with machines and algorithms (AI) on average increasing their contribution to specific tasks by 57% . For example, in the future, 62% of organization's information and data processing and information search and transmission tasks will be performed by machines compared to 46% today.

Therefore, these high technological skillful job change will bring negative influence to some demotive-skillful or low skillful labors to be dismissed, if they can not upgrade or raise or reskillgul their skill level to improve their analytical thinking , technology design and programming skills to cooperate with (AI) tools to work efficiently together in any organizational manufacturing or offie work environment. Because it will have many employers apply (AI) automation tools to participate with blue -color or whiate -color workers' tasks in order to raise efficiencies or improve performance in any working environment. So, it is right time to young or mid age employees need to upskill and/or reskill their rihgt type of skills to prepare future technology risch work environment changeing needs.

Future technological advances will permit an increasing number of tasks traditionally performed by humans to become automated. It seems that , such automation focused primarily on routine tasks, e.g. clerical work, bookkeeping, basic paralegal work and reporting etc. However, with the advent of big data, artificial intelligence (AI), the internet of things and ever-increasing computing power , i.e. the digital revolutions, non-routine tasks are also increasingly likely to become automated. For example, the recent development in robotics and 3D printing allow firms in advanced economies to locate production closer to domestic markets in fully aumomated factories. As a result, the future strongest incentive to automate because of their relatively higher labour costs will be reduced, when production automated will bring the negative influence to dismiss some foolish or low produtive or low skill workers , the owning high automated productive skillful workers will replace the low productive skillful workers in any factories' manufacturing environments. So, technological progress participates to raise quantity of jobs will cause result in significant job losses to low skillful workers. Because future employers will need many high automated productive employees to help them to cooperate with (AI) automated machine to work together efficiently. For example, many proportion of occupations at high risk is greatest in Germany and lowest in Korea, these countries organizations will accept to spend technology investments and education of workers to prepare future automatability manufacturing development successfully.

However, future automatability manufacturing development will bring technological unemployment in possible, due to workers need to adjust to the challenge of automation by switching tasks. Thus, preventing technological unemployment, also technological change does not just destroy jobs, but also generates new roles through its effect on productivity and the demand for new technologies. For example, it has been estimated that, for each high tech-job created in the industries , such as computing equipment or electrical machinery, some 4.9 % additional jobs are created for lawyers, taxi, drivers and waites in the local economy (Moretti, 2011).

Therefore, automated will also influence service industries' job nature change, e.g. taxi drivers need to apply (AI) automated machines to assist them to drive their taxis. When the passenger tells the taxi driver where he/she wants to go. Then, the (AI automated machine will follow the GPS road direction map to be indicated how to drive the taxi to go to the destination automatically . So, future taxi driver is one assistance role to assist the (AI) automated driving tool to dominate the (AI) tool to drive the taxi to catch the passenger to arrive the destination safety in the short time in possible. For another example, future restaurant waiters will need (AI) automated machines's assistance to help them to deliver or dispatch any foods and soft drinks to send to the identified eater's table carefully in accurate and efficient service performance way from the kitchen, in especially in the busy time and many people are sitting in the large size restaurant environment. So, future, waiter roles will be the leader , they need to manage or control or supervise the (AI) robotics how to make decisions to arrange to dispatch which foods or soft drinks to the different tables in preference immediately. Also, future law clerks need to supervise or manage the law robotics how to help them to make decisions to do revision or draft or filing legal tasks in preference in order to avoid any typing words are mistaken to type on computers or revised draft in wrong way to assist manual legal clerks' mistaken words are appearanced on any legal documents. So, the law clerk future role will be the trainer role , he/she eeds to teacher the robots how to check any words, e.g. grammers to correct them to be right grammers, or giving the accurate revision legal documents' instruction to let the legal robots to know how to revise each legal draft to prove whether which part of the legal draft will have wrong to be needed to revise.

In conclusion, future many manual workers' service or manfacturing job natures will become automated assistance to robotics. So, employees need to upgrade their skills in order to adopt new technological work nature change.

Reference

Moretti, E. (2011) local labor market in O, Ashentelter and D. Card (eds.) handbook of labor economics, Elsevier, North Halland.